SEDUCTION AND THE
SECRET POWER OF WOMEN

SEDUCTION

and the

SECRET POWER
OF WOMEN

The Lure of Sirens and Mermaids

Meri Lao

Translated from the Italian by
John Oliphant of Rossie
in collaboration with the author

Park Street Press
Rochester, Vermont

Park Street Press
One Park Street
Rochester, Vermont 05767
www.ParkStPress.com

Park Street Press is a division of Inner Traditions International

Originally published in Italian under the title *Le Sirene: da Omero ai pompieri*
    by Antonio Rotundo Editore in 1985
First U.S. edition published in 1998 by Park Street Press under the title *Sirens: Symbols of Seduction*
First U.S. paperback edition published in 1999 by Park Street Press
Second U.S. edition published in 2007 by Park Street Press under the title *Seduction and the Secret
    Power of Women: The Lure of Sirens and Mermaids*

Library of Congress Cataloging-in-Publication Data
Franco-Lao, Méri.
    [Sirene. English]
  Seduction and the secret power of women : the lure of sirens and mermaids / Meri Lao ; translated
from the Italian by John Oliphant of Rossie in collaboration with the author. — 2nd U.S. ed.
    p. cm.
  Rev. ed. of: Sirens. 1998.
  Includes bibliographical references and index.
  ISBN-13: 978-1-59477-201-6 (pbk.)
  ISBN-10: 1-59477-201-0 (pbk.)
  1. Mermaids. 2. Sirens (Mythology) I. Franco-Lao, Méri. Sirens. II. Title.
  GR910.f6713 2007
  398.21—dc22

                                                                                2007020886

Printed and bound in India by Replika Press Pvt. Ltd.

10 9 8 7 6 5 4 3 2 1

Text design by Rachel Goldenberg
This book was typeset in Garamond, with Cezanne and Gill Sans used as the display typefaces

Grateful acknowledgment is made to the following for permission to reprint these excerpts:

"Lul de Fantenin," by Guillaume Apollinaire, tr. Jon Graham, translation © 1997 by Inner Traditional
    International.
"The Silence of the Sirens," in *The Great Wall of China,* by Franz Kafka, tr. Willa and Edwin Muir,
    translation © 1970 by Schocken Books, New York.
"The Skin," by Curzio Malaparte, tr. David Moore, © 1988 by The Marlboro Press, Marlboro, Vermont.
The Siren and Selected Writings, by Giuseppe Tomasi di Lampedusa, tr. Archibald Colquhoun, ©
    Giangiacomo Feltrinelli Editore 1961, © Archibald Colquhoun, William Collins Sons and Co. Ltd.,
    and Pantheon Books, Inc., 1961, 1962.
Frontispiece: "Ulysses and the Siren," by Friedrich Preller the Younger, Museum der Bildenden Kuenste,
    Leipzig, Germany. Courtesy Erich Lessing/Art Resource, NY.

Contents

Prologue   ix

Introduction   1

1 Classic Sirens   58

2 Fish-Formed Sirens   93

3 An Anthology of Sirens   145

4 Sirens and Science   180

5 Modern Sirens   201

Bibliography   212

Index   222

To Federico Fellini,
de-monstrator of monsters, himself a Siren.

Prologue

Sirens have long been symbols of the lure of desire—the feminine, as seducer—beckoning men to mystery beyond their ken, or to disaster. Since antiquity they and their mermaid sisters have maintained an ongoing affair of the heart with humanity's greatest writers and artists. In his book *Arcane 17,* named after the 17th card of the tarot's Major Arcana (the Star), André Breton invokes the quintessential French Siren Melusine, "the lost woman who sings in man's imagination." This half woman, half serpent holds the key to mysteries unique to women that remain inaccessible to men unless they go through her. Like her sisters, the Lorelei of the Rhine, the Sirens of Greek myth, the merrow of Ireland, undines, and mermaids, Melusine is a supernatural figure that incorporates two different biological entities. It is this figure that Breton appealed to as the only one capable of "redeeming this savage time."

Significantly, this fusion of women and other biological entities can be with the bird, the serpent, or the fish. All three animals are historically associated with secret wisdom, such as the salmon in Celtic myth that eat the hazelnuts which fall from the tree of knowledge and therefore possess all the wisdom in the world. The earliest Sirens were half bird rather than half fish, and thus could speak the language of the birds, which is the tongue of hermetic and esoteric wisdom. But as women became identified with demonic forces, the serpent's body replaced the Siren's wings—another entity banished from its formerly privileged position in the great Mystery traditions to the role of Satan's ally in Christianity.

The winning of esoteric knowledge is at great peril as shown by the story of Lilith in the Hebrew scriptures and by Homer's tale of Ulysses and the song of the Sirens. As does the snake in the Garden of Eden, the Sirens try to seduce Ulysses with knowledge of "everything that happens on the fruitful earth." The price they require, as was the case with Adam and Eve, is death.

In *Seduction and the Secret Power of Women,* Meri Lao shows this death is not so much physical but a transformation of one's former state of existence. The fear inspired by Sirens and mermaids is that of the unknown, of losing oneself or disappearing. Sirens and mermaids urge men to abandon who they are and desert the established order, to leave the world of reason and logic, the domain of men, for the aqueous world of imagination and rebirth ruled by women.

Sirens and mermaids represent the prototypical woman who has been deprived of her rightful place in humanity, as Breton says in *Arcane 17,* "because of Man's impatience and jealousy." In Jewish tradition, Lilith, Adam's first wife and his equal partner, was just this kind of woman. Expelled to make way for a more submissive Eve, Lilith was transformed into an owl (another symbol of wisdom) and "condemned" to haunt the night. Sirens and mermaids combining human aspects with those of bird, fish, or serpent (another cult animal of Lilith) are all daughters of Adam's exiled first wife, making available—to those who dare—the treasures of their mother's wisdom.

JON E. GRAHAM
EDITOR

Introduction

Early Literary and Iconographic Sources

Homer neglected to describe them physically; to have done so would have been superfluous because everyone knew then what later was forgotten: the Sirens were bird-women. Buxom, winged, and sometimes bearded, they almost always had the talons of birds of prey, less frequently lions' paws, and on very rare occasions lower bodies in the form of an egg. When the Sirens' irresistible chant—their supreme attribute—required

John William Waterhouse, *Ulysses and the Sirens*, 1891.
National Gallery of Victoria, Melbourne.

Siren found atop a large funerary monument on the island of Manara. Louvre, Paris. Photo by Chuzeville, 1997.

the musical accompaniment of the lyre, cymbals, or drums, they acquired human arms to hold their instruments.

With wings spread or folded, the earliest Sirens were depicted looming over warriors on the march or sailors at sea. Later they were sculpted on funerary stelae, tearing their flowing tresses and beating their breasts: gestures of distress, bringing to mind professional mourners chanting funeral dirges to comfort afflicted souls.

Not even the simplest ancient Greek would have confused them with the other winged female figures populating the myths and legends of their times, such as Eurynome, who, in the form of a dove, delivered

Annibale Carracci, *Ulysses and the Sirens;* engraving by Pietro Acquila, 1692.
Cartographic Archives of Rome.

the cosmic egg; Nemesis, who punished excess, whether good or evil, and distributed justice; or Eos, who arrived with the dawn to loosen the embrace of lovers.

Nor would the Sirens have been confused with the Harpies, though bodily they resembled them. Both were the issue of a sea god, and both were dedicated to the task of carrying off the dying. The mere thought of encountering the Harpies—cawing and ravenous, dripping their putrid excretions over sumptuously laid tables—inspired horror and loathing. But who among the Greeks did not imagine, at least for an instant, yielding to the enchantment of the Sirens? Who never thought they heard a voice at sea, dulcet and ravishing, instilling a languor of such absolute pleasure as to satisfy all longing?

Literature's first reference to a mortal encountering these supernatural beings is found in Homer's ancient sea epic, the *Odyssey,* created around 800 B.C. The protagonist, Ulysses, was already hardened to the extraordinary apparitions he'd encountered on his way and was skilled as few others in using his wits to circumvent established rules and deceive his adversaries. What is more, Ulysses' watchful ally was Circe herself, a remarkable sorceress and a worthy match for the Sirens in using charm and knowing the secrets of the seas and the otherworld.

It was she who guided him, as captured in Alexander Pope's famous translation:

> *Next, where the Sirens dwell, you plough the seas;*
> *Their song is death, and makes destruction please.*
> *Unblest the man, whom music wins to stay*
> *Nigh the cursed shore, and listen to the lay.*
> *No more that wretch shall view the joys of life,*
> *His blooming offspring, or his beauteous wife!*
> *In verdant meads they sport; and wide around*
> *Lie human bones that whiten all the ground:*
> *The ground polluted floats with human gore,*
> *And human carnage taints the dreadful shore.*
> *Fly swift the dangerous coast; let every ear*
> *Be stopp'd against the song! 'tis death to hear!*
> *Firm to the mast with chains thyself be bound,*
> *Nor trust thy virtue to the enchanting sound.*
> *If, mad with transport, freedom thou demand,*
> *Be every fetter strain'd, and added band to band.*

Ulysses with his face turned toward the ship's mast and his feet in the air, Sirens accompanying their song on the tambourine and lyre; Luccanesque pot with red figures, Paestum, ca. 330 B.C. Staatliche Museum of Berlin.

Circe's wise counsel, which Ulysses would scrupulously follow, enabled him to continue his homeward voyage unscathed. Had he ignored her advice, Ulysses and his crew surely would have gone to join the heap of unburied "human gore" described by Homer, for the price of listening to the Sirens' song was death. Drawn by an unearthly music that swayed the senses, men abandoned their course and threw themselves into the waters to get closer to the sound. Their unguided ships crashed onto the rocky shore.

Homer's Ulysses narrates this episode in flashback before Alcinous, the king of Phaeacia. The most detailed part of the tale is told in the form of a warning to his fellow mariners. Ulysses faces this awesome encounter alone. The sailors, rendered deaf, are occupied with lowering the sails, rowing, and tightening the ropes that bind their captain:

> *Hear and obey; if freedom I demand,*
> *By every fetter strain'd, be added band to band.*
> *While yet I speak the winged galley flies,*
> *And lo! the Siren shores like mist arise.*
> *Sunk were at once the winds; the air above,*
> *And waves below, at once forgot to move:*
> *Some demon calmed the air and smooth'd the deep,*
> *Hush'd the loud winds, and charmed the waves to sleep.*
> *Now every sail we furl, each oar we ply:*
> *Lash'd by the stroke, the frothy waters fly.*
> *The ductile wax with busy hands I mould,*
> *And cleft in fragments, and the fragments roll'd:*
> *The aerial region now grew warm with day,*
> *The wax dissolved beneath the burning ray;*
> *Then every ear I barr'd against the strain,*
> *And from access of frenzy lock'd the brain.*
> *Now round the masts my mates the fetters roll'd,*
> *And bound me limb by limb with fold on fold.*
> *Then bending to the stroke, the active train*
> *Plunge all at once their oars, and cleave the main.*

While to the shore the rapid vessel flies,
Our swift approach the Siren choir descries;
Celestial music warbles from their tongue,
And thus the sweet deluders tune the song:
"Oh stay, O pride of Greece! Ulysses stay!
Oh cease thy course, and listen to our lay!
Blest is the man ordain'd our voice to hear,
The song instructs the soul, and charms the ear.
Approach! thy soul shall into raptures rise!
Approach! and learn new wisdom from the wise!
We know whate'er the kings of mighty name
Achieved at Ilion in the field of fame;
Whate'er beneath the sun's bright journey lies.
Oh stay, and learn new wisdom from the wise!"
Thus the sweet charmers warbled o'er the main;
My soul takes wing to meet the heavenly strain;
I give the sign, and struggle to be free:
Swift row my mates, and shoot along the sea;
New chains they add, and rapid urge the way,
Till, dying off, the distant sounds decay:
Then scudding swiftly from the dangerous ground,
The deafen'd ear unlock'd, the chains unbound.

Once the dangerous territory has been passed, all are safe. The return of Ulysses is guaranteed by the gods, just as it had been when he entered Hades to find the shade of his mother, Anticlea. The sailors were saved simply because they patiently kept their ears stopped up with wax.

The *Argonautica* of Apollonius of Rhodes describes an encounter between the Sirens and another mortal, Orpheus. Among those on the ship *Argo*, on its expedition in search of the Golden Fleece, were Laertes, Ulysses' father, and Peleus, the father of Achilles. Consequently, this episode would predate Homer's by a generation, despite the fact that it was written approximately five centuries later.

Orpheus was an accomplished musician, neither hero nor demigod

Ulysses' ship between the rocks of the Sirens who sing and play the lyre and aulos among the lime-encrusted bones of their previous victims. Behind them is the outline of a large island, possibly Circe's; fresco in Pompei, first century. British Museum.

like the other members of the expedition. He had the task of marking the cadence of the ship's rowers with his lyre. Before they set sail, the centaur Chiron predicted that Orpheus's musical skill would win over the sea enchantresses, and this came to be. Upon reentering the Mediterranean, after crossing the sands of the Libyan desert and recovering the treasure, the Argonauts passed close to the fateful island. At the approach of Anthemoessa, Jason and his companions heard the Sirens "who sent forth their lily-like voices: they were fashioned in part like birds and in part like maidens to behold." Orpheus struck a chord so powerful that it

Ulysses naked and bearded, and the Sirens clothed
in tunics and capes; small alabaster urn.
Guarnacci Etruscan Museum, Volterra.

drowned out their chant, but not before Butes, one of his companions,
heard the song of the Sirens and plunged into the waves. Saved by Aphrodite on the western coast of Sicily, Butes became the lover of the goddess and founded the city of Lilybaeum, which today is Marsala.

Ancient iconography would seem to ignore the Argonauts' legend of
Orpheus. It is for the most part concerned with the mythical musician's
love for Eurydice, his descent into the underworld, and the power his
music exercises over all things, animate and inanimate, and does not
show him overcoming the Sirens.

The Homeric episode, on the other hand, finds ample confirmation
in images—Corinthian and Attic vase paintings, Etruscan statuettes,
Hellenistic gems, and Roman sarcophagus reliefs—most often from the
seventh to the third century B.C. Like the Harpies, the Gratiae, and the
Fates, the Sirens are almost always represented in triads and only rarely

in pairs. Ulysses, curly haired and fully bearded, bound to the mast of his ship, is either naked or wears a chiton that barely covers his shoulder and a conical cap. At times he wears the garb of a warrior. Muscles tensed, his attention is completely absorbed by the bird-women. The sailors are shown rowing, either with sails unfurled before the wind, as Apollonius describes, or drawn up, as in Homer's version. The Sirens appear erect, clinging to the cliffs of their rocky and barren island, a far cry from the bard's "flowering field." Unlike literary sources, which attribute their power exclusively to their singing, in the visual arts Sirens are frequently represented playing musical instruments. To us they remain, eternally poised on the rocks, ready to seduce, awaiting the passing of the next traveler.

There is, however, one exception. The scene depicted on the Attic stamnos and preserved in the British Museum is based on a different

Ulysses and the Sirens, one of whom commits suicide;
Attic stamnos, from Vulci, fifth century B.C. British Museum.

tradition, one handed down by Timaeus, Lycophron, Eustathius, and Hyginus, that would have them commit suicide. As with the Sphinx, it had been predicted by the oracle that they would not survive the first man to resist them. Defeated, they would be seized by a self-destructive urge powerful enough to make them forget the function of their wings, and they would fall like deadweight. In fact, in the representation on this famous vase, one of them is seen precipitating headlong toward the sea. But observe the eyes: closed, indicated by two simple lines, as one might draw the eyes of the blind, the sleeping, or those of one who has decided to put an end to her days. The Siren to the left, with wings spread, would seem ready to follow her sister; the one to the right, however, appears unaware of the defeat.

The ancients refer then to at least three cases in which mortals heard the Sirens and survived. Caught defenseless, Butes is rescued from their spell midway through the enchantment, probably unwillingly. The fourth-century *Orphic Argonautica,* a retelling of the *Argonautica* of Apollonius, adds that the suicide of the Sirens was a consequence of Orpheus's triumph but is silent about the details of the encounter. Orpheus obviously did not hear them, intent as he certainly was on drowning out their voices and preventing the shipwreck of the *Argo.* Ulysses, in the end, heard only praises, promises, and the mention of heroic events that were familiar to him because he had been the principal participant. In this Heraclitus supports Homer when he says that the fascination of the Sirens lay "in the narration of experiences, treasures of centuries past."

Unquestionably the iconographic motif ranges widely. Archaeological finds in northern Syria and Palestine include ninth-century B.C. bronze cauldrons with bird-women represented on their handles, identical to those later found in Greece and Etruria. However, it cannot be confirmed that this analogy of image corresponds to an analogy of function. The Sirens—and this has been established—are winged female sea entities who, by seducing man with their incomparable song, distract him from his set course.

The Sirens as Symbols

The Sirens should be thought of as a millennial symbol. They are a site for innumerable traditions and, as such, are charged with a multiplicity of meanings. In the words of J. J. Bachofen (1815–1887) they are "rich in omens." He preferred the symbolic language of antiquity and art as a perfectly reliable—if antiacademic—instrument of knowledge. In his view, there are two paths to every form of knowledge and comprehension. One is long, slow, and difficult, and the other, imagination, is completed with the force and speed of electricity and is an immediate and total understanding of the truth, richer in life and color than that acquired through the intellect. In his introduction to *Mother Right,* Bachofen writes,

> Knowledge is transformed into comprehension only when it succeeds in grasping the origin, the process, and the end. The origin of any development, however, lies in myth. . . . The distinction between myth and history . . . makes no sense and cannot be justified in the context of human development.

Above all, the Sirens are a hybrid: half woman, half animal—or better still, feminine divinities who are also part of the animal order. Two identities coexist, a double nature. They are halved beings with the prerogatives of both their components; irrational entities, perpetually provocative and disturbing.

In the attempt to eliminate human fear through the exercise of reason, Lucretius (98?–55 B.C.) rejects this idea of a combination of two creatures having different temporal characteristics. Bonding two entities with different natures is impossible. In the centaur, for example, the horse is in his prime at three, while the child is not; when the life force of the horse is waning, the human has yet to reach manhood.

Although there will always be those who challenge the existence of the Sirens with equally valid arguments, what is really of interest here is the interior reality they symbolize. In this sense, Dorothy Dinnerstein's opening to *The Mermaid and the Minotaur,* her book on sexual arrangements and human malaise, is revealing:

From a Corinthian aryballos with black figures, second half of the sixth century B.C.
Boston Museum. Drawing by Teubner.

Myth-images of half-human beasts like the mermaid and the minotaur express an old, fundamental, very slowly clarifying communal
insight: that our species' nature is internally inconsistent, that our
continuities with, and our differences from, the earth's other animals are mysterious and profound; and in these continuities, and
these differences, lie both a sense of strangeness on earth and the
possible key to a way of feeling at home here. . . . D. H. Lawrence was
right to complain of the limited role which the animal mystery, the
cosmic—or religious, in the broader sense—impact has for man.

As we know, in the Freudian concept of the symbol, conflicts are
fused in the metaphor of the unconscious, and censorship disguises
enigma. Hybridization, ambivalence, polarity, duplicity, and dualism are

Vase, sixth century B.C. Villa Giulia
Etruscan Museum, Rome. Photograph
by Giovanni Longobardi.

the qualities that in psychoanalysis denote phantasms created by fear. They are also, according to Mircea Eliade (1907–1986), characteristics of the sacred, which is something artists have always intuitively known. This is the irrational reality to which Jurgis Baltrusaïtis (1873–1944) alludes in his studies on the Gothic, and the reality that led Picasso, among others, to explore all the intermediate stages between man and horse in the search for a more complete harmony.

A supernatural force springs from the fusion of two biologically different entities, opposites that embrace and explain practically everything. From what Carl G. Jung (1875–1961) teaches us about alchemy—which, even before psychology, considered the double nature of every "living reality"—there are symbols that materialize on their own account in our dreams, the expression of which is beyond the dimensions of time and

Jean-Francis Auburtin, *Ancient Evening*, 1911; oil on canvas, Paris.

space and in the sphere of the unspecified and unlimited. These symbols therefore possess a numinous character and impress themselves on the general consciousness, disturbing for those minds used to operating within the limits of logic and rationality. Nevertheless, we can suppose that primordial images, sediments of accumulated memory, collective input, have a life of their own, independent of single individuals. As children we dream of animals we have never seen; what matters is that they approach, flee, or threaten; that we are astonished, bewitched, petrified; or that we overcome them.

Theriomorphic symbols have been present since the time of the Paleolithic cave paintings. Every civilization has had its totems and demons. In the ritual dances of native societies, the cries and movements of animals are imitated and, in order to further facilitate identification

Siren with robust wings and a serpentine tail; Bomarzo, fifteenth century.
Photograph by Angela Citterich.

with the animal, dancers disguise themselves in its skin or plumage and can also incarnate the exorcizing hero. The nightmares of people at the mercy of the mysterious and perpetually changing monster continue to recall the mortal struggle between Marduk and Tiamat, the female dragon; between Vishnu and Hayariva; Heracles and the Hydra of Lerna; Oedipus and the Sphinx; Bellerophon and the Chimera; Perseus and Medusa; and, of course, between Ulysses and the Sirens.

The fusion of human and feral aspects is an emblem venerated in the most ancient religions. Examples include the winged spirits in the Assyrian sculpture in Nimrod, the Babylonian demon Labartu, and the animal-headed stone representations of the Egyptian divinities: Sekmet (lioness), Hathor (cow), Bast (cat), Thoth (ibis), and Horus (falcon). In those cultures in which faith resided in metempsychosis, the destinies of humans and animals were considered indivisible, as both were believed to be temporary dwelling places of the soul. A sizable portion of the beliefs and folklore of the entire planet includes references to human beings transformed into animals and vice versa. Voluntary and involuntary, permanent and alternative metamorphosis: woman by day, deer by night; man by day, wolf by night.

An intermediate being takes form in the Sirens, sweeping aside ephemeral criteria of demarcation and signaling an interruption in the passage from one individuality to another. One of the many possible stages of metamorphosis has been crystallized. Animal connotations are harbored in the images of these mutant women. Sometimes the human aspect is limited to the face, the rest gallinaceous. Other images show a woman's form down to the navel, a bird's from the thighs down; or fine arms and wings, with just the ankles terminating in claws. The frontier between one species and another can suddenly retreat or advance imperceptibly and can vary in infinite ways, toward harmony or jarring contrast. It can be sublime or brutal, generating a procession of new creatures, expressions of tension and obsession, provoking unusual concatenations and inconceivable reactions. "Celestial" animals by constitution, the Sirens are a connection between earth and the heavens, a harbinger of the gods.

David Delamare, *Siren with Mask*, 1983.

In the most disparate cultures, beliefs persist that birds transport the dead on their wings, that during the passage souls take on the appearance of winged creatures, and that those birds that never alight or come to rest are the souls of the damned. Hermes dons winged sandals as he accompanies souls into the realm of death. The perfect soul must have wings if it is not to be trapped in its terrestrial form and forced to undergo the cycle of reincarnation, as Plato (428–347 B.C.) conceived in his *Phaedrus* when he says that the only pasture suitable to the finest part of the anima is in the fields above, where the feathers and plumes that lighten the soul draw nourishment.

For the Toltecs, hummingbirds were the incarnations of warriors killed in battle. Along the Mediterranean coast, seagulls were considered to be the souls of sailors lost at sea. Nobles of many countries believe that when a bird hovers over their lands, someone in their family is about to die. Many native peoples still associate the shamanic trance—the paranormal experience, the leaving of the body—with animals that fly.

The Egyptians were convinced that souls were transported by Thoth, the sacred ibis, and when they depicted the hawk on a tomb, they meant to represent the double, the *koi. Ba,* the soul, was the portrait of the deceased in bird form. The goddesses Maat and Isis, members of the tribunal of the afterlife, open enormous albatross wings in gestures of protection. Five thousand years ago, the Sumerians symbolized both the god Zu and the departed spirits of simple mortals as bird-men, traditionally with feathered wings. Another example is provided by the bronze statue in the Louvre of the Neo-Assyrian winged demon Pazuzu, which dates back to the time of Homer. In *Gilgamesh,* the most ancient epic poem in existence, Eabani is allowed to enter the underworld thanks to a suit of feathers. Wings with eyes speed the Lars, the female spirits of the Etruscans, on their missions of accompanying the dead to their final resting place. Thanatos, the Greek god of death, appears together with his retinue of winged kinsmen: Hypnos (sleep), with his thousands of children, including Morpheus (dream), and Oneiro, his youthful form.

In ancient Rome, an eagle was set free when an emperor died. The eagle, also the emblem of the Roman legions, was believed to carry the emperor's soul heavenward. Birds have been a constant element in the legends of coastal populations that place life after death in those mysterious areas beyond the sea's horizon, to where they believe the souls of the dead migrate. It is worth remembering that in the Germanic languages the words *sea (see, sjo, zee)* and *soul (seele, sjel, ziel)* have the same root.

Thus, we have the first motifs surrounding the symbol of the Sirens: the fatal enchantment, the sacred, instability of form, ambivalence, and transcendental experience. And this is only the beginning.

The island of the Sirens; engraving, 1571. Bibliotheque Nationale, Paris.

The Sirens are midday demons. That is, they act during the hour of ancient religiosity, the pagan hour of phantasms: that shadowless moment at which the sun, at its zenith—when its effect on the earth is most powerful—has ended its ascent and begins its voyage toward night. Its rays, refractive, sparkle on the waters: sunstroke bringing delirium, visions, dog-day drought. Heat softens the wax in the ears of those who must not hear. One alone will gaze at the sun and become illuminated, enlightened.

The Sirens do not pursue. Their territory is well defined—an island in the Tyrrhenian Sea, Anthemoessa, a flowering field near the entrance to the otherworld. The Sirens wait. It is up to men to approach this garden, Eden, paradise. But like the territory inhabited by the Sphinx, it appears strewn with corpses. Flesh-stripped bones and decayed skin provide a stern warning. It is up to men to keep their distance.

Jean-Pierre Vernant, remarking on the image of death in the various myths, literature, and figurative arts, notes that death in the masculine sense, symbolized by Thanatos, signifies the passing away of the hero in the flower of his youth, eternally beautiful, while death in the feminine sense is characterized by the corpse, decomposition. In that case,

Sirens would not be linked to dry dog days but to the humid scirocco, the midday wind, which accelerates the processes of fermentation and depression.

For British author Robert Graves (1895–1985), the Sirens resemble the Stymphalian birds destroyed by Heracles during his sixth labor. Graves considers them morbid, fever-bearing swamp birds. One also notes the presence of musical instruments such as drums and bells, which continue to be used in rituals by native populations to drive off the spirits of fever.

However, the decaying female aspect of the Homeric Sirens was temporarily forgotten during the classical age. In many grave sculptures they are shown beating their breasts with gestures of mourning and lamentation. They became mitigators of death, compassionate creatures sharing in the suffering of those in mourning for their dead, as doleful and lyrical as Euripides found them. And thus they appear once more on the sepulchres of Menander and Sophocles, while the enormous bronze Siren on the tomb of Isocrates, spoken of by Philostratus, has been lost. In compensation, others have been discovered in the necropolises of Myrina and Dypilon: in terra-cotta, the Siren's right hand in her hair and left on her breast; and in marble, tracing the plumed softness, the proud countenance recalling the sculpture of Praxiteles, a fragment of tortoiseshell the only trace remaining of the lyre she holds.

Sonorous epiphany, sweet, honeyed, mellifluous voices—the pleasure of the Sirens lies in hearing their sound. Is it not perhaps because Homer was blind that the eye is rendered useless before their mystery? They exert a primordial quality of seduction: the voice, the words chanted and enchanting. Thus, Plato compared the music of the Sirens to the locution of Socrates, and it would not be difficult to imagine Ulysses, as he twists and turns desperately in the attempt to loosen his bonds, experiencing regret similar to that of Alcibiades, at the height of his power, before the Athenian master:

Under the effect of his discourses, I have often had the impression that it was not worth living. However, it is by force, like one before

Marble tombstone Siren copied from an Attic model. Louvre, Paris. Photograph by Chuzeville, 1997.

the Sirens, stopping my ears to escape the danger, that I flee, otherwise I would become old seated beside him.

A fresh breeze accompanied the Sirens in the account of Apollonius, but it might be wiser to heed the warnings of Homer, so well versed in the sacred, when he speaks of becalmed seas and placated winds.

Ebb tide, parching heat, dog days: the worst conditions for sailing. Rowing becomes an exhausting effort. Sails must be lowered, all activity abandoned and replaced by inaction, stagnation. Time appears suspended in one ecstatic moment. Everything is pervaded by an inexpressible sensation of premonition and rapture. And it is at that moment that the miracle occurs.

Gabriele D'Annunzio (1863–1938) would later exalt that particular moment, midday, the hour of the most intense conjunctions, to be lived through in every aspect "tacit as death." James Hillman connects the tremulousness and splendor of noontide with the god Pan and the spontaneity of instinct; each coincides with its own shadow and tells us that we are beyond the natural order.

Creatures of the air, the Sirens have mastery over space and the summits and the faculty of rising in flight to the heavens. The wing challenges the laws of gravity. The lightness of the feather implies the speed of a whiplash—sail, glide, vanish, hover in the ether. Air brings to mind soul, aura, voices rising, hymn. Bathing in the celestial element of light, the Sirens epitomize purity, ascension, enlightenment: the inaccessible, the divine.

~

Sirens have never been reputed to capture women, which may be explained by the fact that women rarely set off on sea voyages. Had they done so, considerably more balanced accounts of the Sirens would undoubtedly have reached us regarding the essence of feminine wisdom. Instead, it has always been men who told of Sirens, men who dreamed of them, projected onto them, were attracted to and frightened by them. To be consistent with this masculine perspective, only he who has dared to abandon himself and his history, to hurl himself into the deep and sprout wings, emerging into a new life, can hear them.

Homer's attention is mainly absorbed by the mantic abilities of the Sirens. They know "whate'er beneath the sun's bright journey lies." They offer men memory, meaning, knowledge of the world, glory, and fame. And the Greeks—as Giorgio Colli (1917–1979) taught us—considered knowledge the most valuable of worldly achievements: in it every action is reflected and converges. "Blest is the man ordain'd our voice to hear, / The song instructs the soul, and charms the ear," the Sirens tell Ulysses. They render man happy and fulfilled by making him knowledgeable. They tempt him by promising to gratify his lust, provide him with supreme refreshment, and lead him to the ultimate adventure. In other words, they offer to make him immortal, a god. To do this, he has to be diverted, prevented from returning to the same old beaten paths: to past experiences, nation, family, institutions. Sirens are the opposite of the repose of the warrior, the alternative to the sheltered port.

Like that of Dionysus, their effect on man is direct, without intermediaries. Sirens are divinities who fulminate with the knowledge of extreme opposites and could thus be considered the female equivalent of the god of inebriation. Indeed, according to the tradition of Argolis, Dionysus arrived from Naxos with Ariadne by sea, accompanied by the Sirens. But Homer does not mention Dionysus and is not expansive in translating the message of the Sirens into his hexameters. For him, supreme pleasure lies in narrating events already the subject of the *Iliad* and now recounted in the *Odyssey,* roads familiar to him, his past, his universe.

By nature ambivalent, the Sirens maintain an airy quality while at the same time personifying water, the element that, perhaps more than any other, expresses ambivalence. Water has a dual action. It can be a blessing as it slakes the thirst of man, irrigates the earth, and becomes a source of life and abundance, the primordial soup; it represents purification, regeneration, and perpetuity. However, it can also be destructive, causing inundation, shipwreck, drowning, and annihilation. All the vital processes take place in aqueous substances: amniotic fluid is the medium through which we come into the world, and in Greek mythology four rivers provided passage to the underworld. Sirens embody the combination of all these meanings, consequently they are the dispensers of both death and immortality.

In their ambiguity and contradiction, Sirens anticipated the philosophies of multiplicity and becoming that emerged between the seventh and the sixth centuries B.C. in the teachings of Thaletes, for whom the sea, perpetually in motion, is the primal matter; and Anaximander, who saw birth as the separation from the indistinct and death as the return to it. But mainly the Sirens are the forerunners of Heraclitus (576–480 B.C.), he who both suffered for and empathized with humanity, for whom everything was in a state of flux *(panta rei),* and who perceived the coincidence and mediation of opposites:

> Within us the dead and the living, the waking and the sleeping, the young and the old, are the same, since these things, in changing, are those and those, in their turn, are these.

The quality of Becoming is implicit in the element of water, just as the quality of Being is implicit in the element of air. Static, the Sirens attract men, those simple terrestrial creatures, and propel them toward change, the essential passage from one space to another, from one

Gustav Adolf Mossa, *The Sated Siren*, 1905. Nice Gallery.
Photograph by Michel de Lorenzo.

condition to another. Sirens are linked to transit, transitions, transcendence, transfer, long sea voyages, and subsequently to mysteries of initiation—collective in the *Argonautica,* individual in the *Odyssey.* The departure might become a passing away. Let us take the words of Gaston Bachelard (1884–1962) in a flowing reverie from *Water and Dreams:*

> Death is a journey, and a journey is a death. "To leave is to die a little." To die is truly to leave, and no one leaves well, courageously, cleanly, except by following the current, the flow of the wide river. All rivers join the River of the Dead. This is the only mythical death, the only departure that is an adventure.

Ulysses and Orpheus have this adventure in common as well. The katabasis, the descent into Hades, is completed by Ulysses just prior to his encounter with the Sirens, and awaits Orpheus long after his triumph over the bird-women. The knowledge of the Sirens belongs to the marine element and thus is prophetic and secret. "The old men of the sea," as Homer called the ancient sea gods, knew everything, saw beneath, through, and beyond. The only problem for those who aspired to obtain a response from them was to succeed in holding them still, because another of their extraordinary capacities was to suddenly assume the most unexpected forms. Oceanus, Achelous, Pontus, Phorcus, Nereus, Poseidon, and—by definition—Proteus were protean. Transient and relative, they were indeterminate and amorphous. Like water, these gods were generators of polymorphism, transformations, metamorphoses, and new identities. One rash movement, a sudden quickening, sufficed for the unpredictable and elusive animal to appear.

Likewise, the Sirens call to man, urging him to abandon what he is, to become a transgressor; fear of the Sirens is the fear of upsetting the established equilibrium, of transforming, of being replaced, even in part, by something unpredictable; fear of the unknown, of losing oneself, disappearing or dissolving. Returning to Bachelard's chain of thought, if the dissolution of the earth ends in dust and fire ends in smoke, the dissolution of water is yet more radical:

Water dies with the dead in its substance. Water is then a *substantial nothingness*. No one can go further into despair than this. For certain souls, *water is the matter of despair.*

Genealogy, Relationships, Affinities

Even the genealogy of the Sirens offers material for further symbolic speculations. The father usually attributed to the Sirens is Achelous, the oldest water divinity of the West, who today is associated with the river Aspropotamus, which descends from the Pindus Mountains to flow through the lands of Aetolia. On ancient vases, he is depicted with a long, curved fish tail, engaged in a struggle with Heracles for the possession of Deianeira or kneeling before the father of the contested maiden and next to his rival in love. One important detail: Heracles had just reemerged from the underworld where he had completed the twelfth of his labors. When the struggle explodes between the two suitors, Achelous changes into a bull, having decided to fully exploit his prerogative to set his adversary off balance. Heracles, however, succeeds in defeating him by tearing off one of his horns. Immune to decay, the horn became the origin of the cornucopia, and the drops of divine blood spilled generated the Sirens.

Like the Sirens, the goddesses Athena and Aphrodite were born without woman. The former, as we know, emerged from the head of Zeus, aided by Hephaestus, who dealt him a skillfull blow with an ax. Aphrodite took form from the genitals of Uranus, which had been severed and thrown into the sea by his son Cronus, goaded by his mother, Gaea, who also provided him with the weapon. Yet again, birth from the pain of a defeated god, his masculine attributes mutilated.

Athena, however, differs from the Sirens in her practical and prudent wisdom and her assiduous protection of Ulysses, her favorite among mortals. Aphrodite presents greater similarities in her magnetism, sometimes in her physical aspect, and later in certain traits that provided the fabric for popular legend. She emerged from an island, maintained close ties with the destiny of navigators, possessed the ability to placate the

The battle between Achelous and Heracles; Attic vase. The British Museum.

winds, had a sacred friendship with dolphins, and—only much later—was known for her erotic appeal.

The maternal genealogy of the Sirens is controversial. Generally, the Muses are considered to be the mothers of the Sirens, having coupled with Achelous for that purpose. Apollonius believes their mother to be Terpsichore, the goddess of the dance. Hyginius points at Melpomene, the goddess of tragedy. For some it was Sterope, and for others, Calliope, the goddess of eloquence, the bearer of musical genes; many texts also present her as the probable mother of Orpheus, as well as the unquestioned mother of Linos, the inventor of melody and rhythm. Some believe the Sirens to be stepsisters of the Muses, being the product of a union of Achelous and Mnemosyne—memory—who had spent nine nights with Zeus to conceive the nine goddesses. Euripides thought the Sirens to be born of Mnemosyne's daughter Gaea. Thus, once more they are linked to that subterranean and occult divinity who had been forced by her husband, Uranus, to keep secret the children in her womb.

A different paternity is suggested by Plato, who considered the Sirens to be the issue of the union of Phorcus and his sister Cetus, the whale. If this were true, the Sirens would be the stepsisters of terrible monsters such as Echidna, Scylla, the Gorgons, and the serpent who guarded the golden apples that lay underground. According to numerous other sources that identify the Sirens with the Nereids, their progenitor would be Nereus, brother—or perhaps father—of Phorcus.

In this intricate genealogical jungle, certain constants are nevertheless evident. The father of the Sirens is recognized as a god, which is enough to render them immortal. He is a water god and therefore omniscient and protean, qualities usually passed down to progeny. Figures of the mother almost inevitably possess great affinities to music, memory, and secret wisdom, the very qualities that distinguish the Sirens.

However, we should not completely dismiss the idea that the Sirens were generated without feminine participation. It would be reasonable to imagine them taking form from a fluid element, sea or blood, indistinct and changing, in a succession of derivations, a kind of perpetual self-fertilization. Reversing this process, in *Metamorphoses* Ovid (43 B.C.–A.D. 17) clearly recorded the dissolution of Cyane, a Siceliad, whom others considered a true Siren.

> You should have seen her limbs become slack, the bones pliant, the nails lose their hardness. In the cold water, her most tender parts became liquid first: the black flowing hair, the fingers, the legs, the feet; and then the transformation of her other delicate limbs. Then her shoulders, back, hips, and her breasts dissolved into small streams. And, finally, into the broken veins, in the place of living blood, entered water, until nothing more remained to be grasped.

Water principle, sea matter, primordial matter—first mother. Time and again we see the Sirens associated with materialization and dissolution in any liquid matrix: sea, amniotic fluid, tears. It is perhaps for this reason that their maternal origin is unclear.

What may be more significant are the other feminine figures of an aquatic nature whose destinies are intertwined with that of the Sirens. These tormented creatures, after having sought refuge in the sea, reemerge under other names. One example of these is the Cretan Britomartis ("the sweet virgin") who, seeking to escape the lust of Minos, flung herself into the sea. Rescued by a fisherman, she assumed the names of Dictynna ("from the net") and Aphaia ("the invisible"). Later identified with Artemis, she is honored in Ephesus in the temple considered one of the marvels of the world, where Heraclitus often sought refuge. Cesare Pavese (1906–1950), a writer who also committed suicide, imagined a dialogue between Britomartis and Sappho: the nymph plunged into the sea to save her immortal essence, while Sappho, a mortal, did so simply to disappear.

Similarly, the story of Leucothea ("the white goddess"), the Leucò of Pavese's dialogues, the metamorphosis of Halia or Ino, demonstrates how, in the liquid element, the most horrible crimes connected with maternity can be resolved and exorcised. Halia was one of the wives of Poseidon, a descendent of the family who forged the famous trident.

Mauro Corbani, *The Rape of the Sirens*, 1985; chalk and pencil.
From the author's collection.

After she is raped by Poseidon's six sons, Halia throws herself into the sea. She is then born again as the Siren Leucothea. For Homer, who describes her as a swamp bird emerging from the waters and then disappearing again, she is instead the transformation of Ino, pursued by her husband, Athamas. After she attempts to kill her stepchildren, who were saved by being placed on the back of the ram of the Golden Fleece, Athamas takes his revenge by killing Learchus, one of his sons conceived with her. Ino flees, carrying Melicertes, her youngest child. Exhausted, she flings herself into the sea together with the child. Zeus then changes her into Leucothea, and it is in this form that she will offer to Ulysses a cloak bestowing invulnerability to help him reach the land of the Phaeacians when he is about to be drowned by a furious Poseidon.

At this point in the myths, we are at the height of Olympian domination. Zeus, Pluto, and Poseidon, the three sons of Cronos and Rhea, divide among themselves power over the earth. The latter son nurtures an intense hatred for Ulysses, who caused the death of his nephew Palaemon and blinded his son Polyphemus. It is clear that only in the absence of Poseidon are the other Olympians able to offer their protection to Ulysses, thus making his extraordinary adventures possible, including his encounter with the enchantresses of the sea.

The Sirens are intent only on attracting passing mortal men with their music. They are not in the least interested in power struggles, even those involving the most eminent of divinities. Probably for that reason they were never in the good graces of the divine arbitrators of contests and wars. They have some similarities with the second generation of Oceanids: with Medea, for the magic arts and the connection with the Argonaut enterprise; with the Harpies and Nike, for their similar physical resemblance; with Narcissus, for their common signifier of the mirror from the Middle Ages on. But they are most analogous to the Nereids, the only nymphs who, like the Sirens, are immortal.

Hesiod (ca. 800 B.C.) counted the daughters of Nereus and Doris as fifty, two of whom, Eumolpe and Ligea, would subsequently be considered Sirens. A constant presence in the legends of Sicily is Galatea, who preferred the love of the shepherd Acis to that of Polyphemus, a tale

Kolo Moser, *The Waves of the Danube;* wallpaper ca. 1890. Grassi Palace, Venice.

immortalized by the painter Raphael (1483–1520) and celebrated by the poet Angelo Poliziano (1454–1494).

Certain connections with the Sirens are to be found in other feminine figures. Arethusa, pursued by the lusty river god Alceus, immersed herself in the waters of Syracusa, her head surrounded by dolphins. Amphitrite—who, in Homer, was "the daughter of the sea" par excellence—though reluctant at first, was pursuaded by a dolphin to mate with Poseidon. Then there is Argila, who so fascinated the young Thrasymenus that he became a lake in order to unite with her. And finally, Thetis, the subdued bride of Peleus and mother of Achilles, foreseeing the death of her son in Troy, attempted to render him invulnerable by plunging him into the waters of the Styx—even though, as we know, the fatal heel remained dry. Thetis led the swarm of Nereids, compared by

Apollonius of Rhodes to seagulls and dolphins, who raised the ship *Argo* as if it were a toy, rescuing it from the fury of the elements unleashed as it left the island of the Sirens.

It is customary to classify the aquatic nymphs according to their habitat. Besides the sea-dwelling Nereids, there were the lake-dwelling Lymneids, the river Potomids, and the Naiads of the springs. These are minor nymphs, long lived but not eternal, although always versed in the most hidden secrets and capable of metamorphosis. Springs are almost always proof of this. Here bubble the waters of Aganippe, and those who drink of them are transformed into poets. There lies Cassotis, who became the source of the oracle at Delphi, conferring gifts of prophecy to the priestesses of Apollo. On Mount Helicon remains Castalia, who climbed there to dedicate herself to the Muses and inspires poetry in those who wet their lips at her source or listen to its murmur.

The attitudes, attributes, and situations of these female figures all appear to belong to the same symbolic universe as the Sirens. However, from Homer to the early Christians, the Sirens were represented as bird-women, while the other aquatic creatures, eternal or otherwise, did not differ physically from mortal women. And in that aspect lies the vital difference. The nymphs, young and beautiful, rejoice in each other's company, sing and dance, and sometimes even spin. Although they dwell in the depths of the sea in palaces of crystal and gold, their hair is dressed and they wear jewelry and clothing not unlike that of their mortal contemporaries. Nor do the nymphs appear to be interbred with animals as were the Satyrs—their male counterparts—or the other males of their species. Neither did the Oceanids who splashed in the waves around their white-bearded, taurine-horned father. The Nereids also resembled mortal women, although they were in close communion with animals to which they provided food and drink, usually panthers, hippocampi, sea dragons, and dolphins, on whose backs they are depicted riding the waves. Only later would nymphs acquire fish tails, as did the Sirens. And it is at this point that the human memory begins to superimpose details, to scramble facts, and to confound.

Sirens and the Incomprehensible Feminine

The Sirens are bird-women. The reasons given to explain their wings shed some light on the profound aspect of the other half of their nature: the female human. Here, too, ambivalence is at work. Born nymphs, the Sirens would obtain wings either as punishment or as a reward. Born winged women, their wings would be clipped for the same reason. In most myths this involved goddesses related to music, love, maternity, and death.

Pausanius, Eustathius, and Julian bring into the story the Muses, who also possess beautiful voices and are musicians and dispensers of wisdom. Here they are no longer mothers to the Sirens but ferocious adversaries instead. At that time possessing wings, the Sirens dared challenge the Muses to a singing contest. The Muses, in order to humiliate them, pitilessly tore off their wings and with them made crowns, now their emblem. Deplumed, mortified, and no longer able to fly, most of the Sirens committed suicide—at least in the opinion of Stephanus of Byzantium. Some, however, resigned themselves to remaining literally roosted on the cliffs, and in this position they would have tbeen sighted by Ulysses and his crew. Although the names and places— Leucothea, Leucosia, Leucadia, Galatea—imply a white epidermis, smooth and unadorned, the existing imagery suggests otherwise, depict-

Contest between the Sirens and the Muses, from a bas-relief on the sarcophagus of the Neri family of Florence, third century.

ing them during the encounter with Ulysses as winged and feathered.

To others, it was Aphrodite who caused them to take bird form, as a sign of their degradation from the superior beings they were. Thus, the goddess of love punished the Sirens' obstinate insistence on remaining virgins and refusing to couple with mortals or even gods. Pierre Grimal writes that this was the destiny of Parthenope alone, a Phrygian girl who, having fallen in love despite her vow of chastity, cut her hair and went into voluntary exile in Campania and dedicated herself to Dionysus. There she was transformed into a Siren by Aphrodite.

A version richer in symbolic meaning associates the Sirens' wings with the myth of Demeter and her daughter, Persephone. Demeter, the goddess of corn and harvests, acts in her basic role of Mother Earth, as the name *Dea Mater* implies. By reaffirming the connection between wings and the underworld, this myth offers some explanation for the feminine enigma and the relationship with birth as well as the eschatological destiny of man.

The Sirens, nymphs accompanying Persephone, were intent on gathering violets and narcisi and generally amusing themselves and did not pay attention when Hades kidnapped the divine maiden, abducting her to his realm in the underworld. Demeter accused them of not having attempted to prevent this and, to punish them, transformed them into birds. Some writers sustain, on the contrary, that they were already birds and were now deprived of their ability to fly as punishment.

The Sirens obtain wings from Demeter in order to go more swiftly in their search for Persephone; French engraving, seventeenth century. Cartographic Archives of Rome.

Howard Pyle, *The Mermaid*, 1910. Delaware Museum of Art.

A more charitable explanation is given by Ovid: the Sirens themselves prayed for wings so that they could fly over the water and spread news of their grief. As Ovid reminds us, Cyane was also part of that group and tried to prevent Persephone's being dragged down into the underworld. When she failed, she merged with the waters in desperation.

Given this ambiguity, we might offer another interpretation of this event. The Sirens were present, as usual, at a transition from the realm of the living to that of the dead, which here involved the maiden of spring, who was to become the queen of the realm of shadows. Consequently, it was a transition they could never have prevented without betraying their own mission. They would, in fact, facilitate it, indifferent as always to quarrels between the gods. Demeter first and foremost a mother, circumvented the laws for her daughter and, consequently, reproached and punished the Sirens.

The Sirens nevertheless maintained close ties with Persephone, interceding with their plaintive singing to procure peace for the dead. This, at least, is the opinion of Euripides (480–406 b.c.); his Helen, deeply distressed by the misdeeds perpetrated in her name, invokes them:

Virgin Sirens, daughters of the earth, gay maidens, accompany my sighs with your lybian flutes and your sad syrinx, like the tears that calamities bring forth in me. Raise to Persephone funereal dirges, offerings bathed by my tears, hymns in honor of the dead, that resound in her shadowy palace.

The rest of the tale of Demeter and Persephone is familiar enough. Demeter, in her grief at losing her daughter, destroyed the harvest. At that point, a definitive return to the earth was no longer possible for Persephone because the maiden had tasted a pomegranate, which bound her to the underworld. Nothing remained but to resort to a divine compromise in which Demeter succeeds in having Persephone spend part of the year above ground with her and part in the realm of the dead with Hades, with whom she never produces offspring.

In Eleusis, the destination of Persephone's long terrestrial pilgrimage, Demeter later had built a temple where men would be initiated into her mysteries. Statues—images of Aphrodite, Hera, Athena, Helen, Maia, Artemis, and Demeter—were immersed in the sea and made to reappear. In a forest of sanctuary columns, novices witnessed various representations; a famous one is the episode of Apelles, who paints Aphrodite rising from the waves, inspired by the interpretation of Phryne. However, it is Persephone who reemerges, in a continuous return, from the waters as a primordial entity. The great lesson of Eleusis was that birth transcended the individual and was capable of canceling the death of every living being and consequently of conferring immortality.

Jung, studying the figures of Kore, the germ of wheat, and of Demeter, the mature spike, confirms once more his theory of the collective unconscious, which would manifest in the form of enigmas, the key to which can be found in the wisdom of antiquity. *Anima* is the Jungian term used to designate the "unknown woman," a figure with a multiplicity of facets who oscillates between goddess and prostitute, young and old, virgin and mother. The description is particularly apt for the Sirens:

> Besides this ambivalence, the Anima has "occult" links with the "mysteries" and in general with the dark world, and thus often assumes a religious tinge. When it appears with a certain clarity it always has a particular relationship with time: frequently it is beyond time; that is, almost or completely immortal.

Plutarch (ca. 46 to after A.D. 119) had already commented on the similarity between the words *teleutan* (to die) and *teleisthai* (to be initiated). In the Eleusinian mysteries, in fact, death was ritually evoked with a miming of the event, inevitably followed by rebirth, bathed in light—the supreme summit of cathartic exaltation. Possessing the secret of eternity, the initiated—as Sophocles (ca. 496–406 B.C.) explained—were freed of anxiety:

Blessed are those mortals who, having contemplated these mysteries, go on to Hades. They alone can continue living there. For the others, all will be torment.

Through the sacred ordeal of the plunge into the sea or the incarceration in the cave of Hecate—the shadow aspect of Demeter and Kore—it was possible to lose the references of time and space and experience a delirium that disintegrated personality. This mania, the state of exaltation, or poetic inspiration, was described by Plato and put into verse by Anacreon (ca. 582–ca. 485 B.C.):

> *Once more, once more*
> *from Leucade's rock I dive*
> *into the sea;*
> *and once more amidst the white foam drunk with love.*

Exposed to this type of experience, the adepts transformed certain abstract images into reality: the "leap in the dark," for example. It is in the dark that the passage from prebirth to birth takes place—in the maternal womb, the embryo, in the earth, the grain of wheat that Persephone represents. In the words of Bachelard:

> In point of fact, the *leap* into the sea, more than any other physical event, awakens echoes of a dangerous and hostile initiation. It is the only, exact, reasonable image, the only image that can be experienced of a *leap* into the unknown. There are no other *real* leaps "into the unknown." A leap into the unknown is a leap into water. It is the first leap of the novice swimmer.

The sea, the womb, Eleusis—all are places of birth and transformation, where the enigma of generation is concealed. Containing all manner of snare and wonder, pleasure and mystery, the dangers of the sea become metaphors for the dangers of the feminine realm. Simone de Beauvoir (1908–1986) was among the first to examine the question.

In the deeps of the sea it is night: woman is the *Mare tenebrarum,* dreaded by navigators of old; it is night in the entrails of the earth. Man is frightened of his night, the reverse of fecundity, which threatens to swallow him up. He aspires to the sky, to the light, to the sunny summits, to the pure and crystalline frigidity of the blue sky; and under his feet there is a moist, warm, and dark gulf ready to draw him down; in many a legend do we see the hero lost forever as he falls back into the maternal shadows—cave, abyss, hell.

The lapping of the waves, "the eternally rocking cradle," taught Walt Whitman the word *death.* According to Géza Roheim (1891–1953), Hungarian exponent of psychoanalytical anthropology, we model our conception of life after death on sleep or dreams. The process of falling asleep could be a prototype of the passage to the otherworld, and waking up the morning after, of resurrection. The accounts of the voyage to the underworld and the subsequent return reveal traces of their oneiric origin: aspects of the fundamental dream of falling into water, which is akin to drowning in the moist vagina. There is a recurrent association: sleep–water–birth–death. In Roheim's thesis, sleep is a periodical regression to the womb, which has a double aspect—desire and fear. The Sirens, a dream that originates from urethral tension, are the projection

Milo Manara, album cover, 1975, Rome.

of the maternal image. The claws indicate the fear of castration; the wings signal erotic prowess.

> The Song of the Sirens is a mother's lullaby. . . . In the depth of the unconscious there must exist an engram of the embryo floating in a liquid, which is unfailingly stimulated by the sight of water. The concept of liquid is also associated with the semen, vaginal liquid, and coitus as sleep, the uterine regression. Coitus together with castration is translated into the Song of the Sirens, while the relaxation following coitus and uterine regression represent Elysium.

Slow-moving waters that precede and follow the moment of birth—amniotic fluid, mother's milk—the fearful anticipation of fathomless waters after death, the ritual leap into the sea, are a condensation of all these possible connections brought to light by authors such as Jung, Erich Neumann, Jacques Bril, Anita Seppilli, and Marie Bonaparte, who states:

> The waters represent the pre-natal mother, that moist place in which we slept before coming into the world. And thanks to the real fact that in diving we could drown and sleep forever, the lethal state after death is assimilated to the fetal state before birth, explaining the mixture of nostalgia and anxiety which takes possession of the human being on the shore: nostalgia of air-breathing creatures for the true real repose which the final leap into the liquid media will bring.

All of these images, each one with its myriad significances and each inspiring both attraction and fear, are implicit in the symbol of the Siren. The sea is capable of killing man but also of rocking him maternally. The womb engulfs man but is also the means of his coming into the world. The Sirens demand that man leap into the unknown but also offer him eternal life.

Sirens and Music

During the Alexandrian period the mystery cults converged: the Eleusinian mysteries, the minor mysteries of Agraea, those founded by Gaea to Hermione and those dedicated to Demeter, those of Samothrace, and the Orphic mysteries, theological metaphor of Dionysian mysteries.

As tradition would have it, Orpheus was the first to experience Hades and live. The intention of the religion that bore his name was to purify the human soul of its terrestrial–Titanic–mortal condition and reveal its astral–Dionysian–immortal aspect. Through the steps of the mysteries, initiates acquired the knowledge of their own astral nature, hastening the reascension of their souls, which would descend into the tomb with their bodies after death. Then, freed from the chain of reincarnation, the souls could be brought before Persephone with the claim of being celestial; she would then welcome them like gods.

Orphism gave great importance to memory: the world is an illusion and only those who remember can ascend once more to the real, immutable world that transcends time. And it is here that Mnemosyne comes into play. She is the goddess who quenched the thirst of the initiates, awakening them to memory, while common souls, forced to repeat the cycle of incarnation, partook of the water of the river Lethe, which offers oblivion, forgetfulness. Did not man in antiquity seek in the mystery religions the very gift that the Sirens—not surprisingly since they were considered daughters of Mnemosyne—could bestow in an instant of ecstasy?

Pythagoras (571–497 B.C.) was one of the great initiates of the Orphic mysteries. For the secret community that bore his name and was persecuted to the point of extermination, the teachings of the master had an axiomatic value; they were formulated on ethical and religious precepts based on the conviction that knowledge is the means to salvation. The fall of the soul—the loss of wings—was explained in astronomical and geometrical terms and with harmonic numbers. A rectilinear trajectory indicated disorder, limits, and a tendency toward immobility in terrestrial bodies. Circular trajectory, on the other hand, suggested uniform and eternal patterns in the stars, and therefore the existence

Gustave Gurschner, oil lamp.

of an intelligent, divine "anima," the "nous," which found its terrestrial correspondence in the human soul.

For the Pythagoreans, music, the sister of astronomy, was the regulator of the constellations—of their course, rhythm, order, and harmony. The moving stars diffused harmony in their spheres. Human music was nothing more than its imitation.

Heraclitus, too, supposed, in his *Allegory of Man,* that those sidereal masses in motion produced sound, which would inevitably be translated into a wise harmony. For Pythagoras, this music was verifiable and enjoyable and, as Giamblico states in his biography of Pythagoras, in the clear Italian nights the philosopher of Samos, in ecstasy, could actually hear the celestial harmonies.

Sounds emitted by the astral bodies, those produced accidentally while striking irons of various measures, and those that Pythagoras and his disciples produced on the monochord for their experiments are all governed by a mathematical relationship between the vibrating material and the frequency of the sound, indicated by fractions. These fractions include the greatest early discoveries in acoustics and are translated into ciphers that the Greeks considered consonance. To express them, only the four first numbers are necessary.

The Tetractys was the sacred formula of the Pythagoreans: on it they vowed never to reveal to the uninitiated the arithmetic and religious truths of their sect. It was expressed as $1 + 2 + 3 + 4 = 10$ and was represented by an equilateral triangle made up of ten points, one central and four per side. The number four was conferred with great powers; it had a universal character because the regions of the heavens and the earth were four. Based on an analogical system, other concepts were associated with the Tetractys and governed by the number four, such as the elements, the phases of the moon, the seasons, the ages of man, the cardinal points, the parts of the soul, four equal sections of a circle, or the circling of the quadrant. The same expression in reverse, $10 = 1 + 2 + 3 + 4$, represented the squaring of the circle.

Being even, the number four is unlimited because it is infinitely divisible, as taught by Philolaus (fifth century B.C.), the first to write on the Pythagoreans. No less important, the Tetractys recalls that succession of four combined sounds known as the tetrachord. The entire Greek musical system—calculated by Pythagoras—was obtained by means of a succession of tetrachords, in descending order.

But what role do the Sirens play in this complicated musical system? A precept of the Oracle of Delphi presents the Tetractys as the harmony existing where the Sirens are found. While for the Pythagoreans the music of man has the mission of rousing the soul in its prison of an earthly body, stimulating love for things divine, the oracular music of the Sirens enflames errant souls with the memory of, or longing for, the heavens and renders definitive detachment painless.

A passage from Plato's *Republic* revealing unmistakable Orphic and Pythagorean connotations associates the music of the Sirens with the doctrine of metempsychosis. This is the narration by Er, a Pamphylian warrior miraculously returned from the dead, of his stay in the world beyond the tomb. First, he alludes to a flowering field that brings to mind Elysium as well as Anthemoessa, where the Sirens kept their watch for seafarers, and the garden where they played together with Persephone before she was dragged into the abyss. After having passed eight days there, groups of the dead set off for four more days, until the vision of a series of linked astral spindles was set before them. The last of the eight, a spindle of diamonds placed in the center of the universe, astonished them with its brilliance. The spindle is turned by Ananke (Necessity), daughter of Cronus and Tyche, the goddess whom Orphism adopted as a primordial mother. She is accompanied by her daughters, the three Fates. Between the four goddesses, placed in perfectly geometrical order, are the eight Sirens, who sing in response to a perfect harmony.

> And the spindle turned on the knees of Necessity, and up on each of the rims of the circles a Siren stood, borne around in its revolution and uttering one sound, one note, and from all the eight there was a concord of a single harmony. And there were three others who sat round about at equal intervals, each one on her throne, the Fates, daughters of Necessity, clad in white vestments with filleted heads, Lachesis, and Clotho, and Atropos, who sang in unison with the music of the Sirens, Lachesis singing the things that were, Clotho the things that are, and Atropos the things that are to be.

At this point, it might be worth making a brief digression concerning the frequency of sound. It is perhaps not by chance that the undeniable consonance for all musical civilizations is the octave and that sounds at intervals of an octave seem so similar as to merit the same name: the eighth note in fact has the same name as the first, after which the series recommences. Indeed, the explanation as to why that "perfect consonance" pleases the human ear is not exclusively cultural preference: the vibrations of sounds separated by an octave have a two to one ratio, and this reflects a law of physics. The possibilities of halving or doubling the

Siren trumpeter with a double tail; lamp post in cast iron on the riverfront of the Neva River, St. Petersburg. Photograph by Giovanni Longobardi, 1996.

frequency would be infinite if our perception were capable of capturing infrasonic and ultrasonic frequencies.

Plato places the Sirens and their music within a vast and cosmogonical, pre-Olympian system, among the feminine entities regulating the destiny of the universe and the human race. Ananke represents the necessary laws of nature; it is she who governs the movement of the spheres and she who determines the number of initial vibrations. The Sirens are the sonorous manifestation of Ananke. But, at the same time, they sing in harmony with the Fates, that is, with the rules regulating the lives of mortals, whose days they spin, wind into a skein, and finally cut.

We can imagine the Sirens, situated at equal distances from the four goddesses and double their number, singing in unison. This recalls Leibniz's explanation in his *New Essays on Human Understanding* that the sound of the sea is made up of an infinity of lesser sounds. This resonance—perhaps bound to luminous phenomena, given the analogy existing between the laws governing sound and those governing light—is so perfect a harmony as to remain eternally fixed, like a carillon under the mountains of sand on the Red Sea coasts, the waterfall on the Chinese river Heng (called the bell), the waves crashing against the basalt walls of the Cave of Fingal, the organlike sounds made by the rocks of the Orinoco, or the melodious crinkling of the colossal statues of Memnon. Whoever hears this sound acquires memory of past and future and of the underlying truths governing them.

Music was defined by Trismegistus as no more than the knowledge of the order of all things. Perfect music: as such, it is made up of Parmenidean time, which does not pass but is always equal unto itself, that mythical, primordial time that we rediscover only during feasts, celebrations, rites. It is a music that is also imperfect if we hold to the simultaneous presence of opposites. And here we might quote Maurice Blanchot's *Le Livre a Venir* (1907), for whom the music of the Sirens is a song "to come," which leads the mariner to the place of origins, to that destination where the song may begin:

> There was something marvellous about this chant, this common, secret, simple and everyday song, which all at once revealed through it the singing of irrational and (why not) imaginary powers, the song of the depths: which, once understood, its every word opening an abyss which powerfully urged one to lose oneself in it. The song (and this is not to be forgotten) was directed at seafarers, courageous men of action, and was itself a voyage: it was distance, but at the same time revealed the possibility of crossing that distance, of making of that song the movement towards song, and of that movement the expression of the most powerful desire. . . . The Sirens [were] defeated by the power of technology, which will always insist on playing without

taking risks with the unreal (inspired) powers, from which Ulysses was not, however, liberated. They lured him to where he did not wish to fall and, hidden in the Odyssey which had become their tomb, they bound him and many others to that happy, unhappy voyage which is the narration: the song, no longer direct, but narrated, is rendered apparently harmless. Ode becomes episode.

Man has always, with every means he possesses, attempted to bury the Sirens, inventing ways to reduce their powers and condemn them to silence, thus denying himself. He did not want them to defeat Ulysses or Butes and even less so the Muses or Orpheus, against whom he had them combat in an exquisitely musical tension. He never placed them on Olympus.

Let us examine more closely the Sirens' encounter with the Muses. Although it was not unusual for the Sirens to be called the "Sea Muses," if we go back to the divinities whence they both originate, we see that they are affiliated with diametrically opposing spheres. The Sirens are placed among the most isolated and remote of the female deities. The Muses, in their function of providing counsel and inspiration, act as intermediaries between a few elect mortals and Apollo. This Greek god succeeded in gathering to him the greatest number of proselytes and presiding over the most varied of activities, including music, navigation, and guiding the path of the sun during its daily journey. As his influence increased, the old sages of the sea and Poseidon himself were left behind. Far-reaching Apollo monopolized the solar space that was the Sirens' realm of direct action. In his capacity as a Muse leader *(Musagetes)*, Apollo directed the chorus of the Muses; as the Delphic Apollo, he fulfilled the oracular function through Pythia. His is an oblique action that is expressed—at least in the Sirens' area of music and prophecy—through the mediation of female entities in ancillary roles.

The Muses, obedient votaries of Apollo, made up the jury in the competition between Marsyas, the satyr flutist devoted to Cybele, and Apollo and his lyre. They decreed Marsyas the loser and decided that he be skinned alive by the victor. Followers of Apollo in all things, even in their methods of punishing the defeated, the Muses rendered the Thracian bard Thamyris dumb and blind for boasting that his talents surpassed theirs. And, as we will remember, the Muses plucked off the wings of the Sirens, making them ridiculous. The plumes stolen from their rivals were used as an ornament and became their emblem. The sea enchantresses fell silent forever, perhaps transformed into mute rocks by their adversaries.

What future destinies were to be decided in that singing contest to have provoked such furious hatred on the part of the victors? According to the Greek geographer Pausanius it was Hera who goaded the Sirens to challenge the Muses, and Zeus who acted as arbiter, which would confirm the thesis that it was a settling of old scores with a pre-Olympian cult. It is hard to disagree with the French scholar Cerquand, who sees the episode as a historic event, a conflict between Roman goddesses (the Sirens) and Greek goddesses (the Muses)—altar versus altar, with all the hatred characterizing religious wars. Regrettably, Cerquand, satisfied that the Muses had the upper hand, also gives high moral significance to the event: victory went to the industrious.

Hesiod does not mention the Sirens in his *Theogony* but begins with the Muses, daughters of Zeus, the god of gods, and Mnemosyne, before whom memory did not exist. Even Pythagoras preferred the Muses:

> There are two kinds of pleasure: the first which is akin to appetites, voluptuousness, wealth, and can be compared to the homicidal songs of the Sirens, and the second which has its origin in beauty, justice, all that which is necessary to life, pleasant at the moment without the residue of remorse, and not unlike the harmony of the Muses.

The Muses sang, played musical instruments, and danced when the gods assembled, leaving their Olympian dwellings to visit the rare, lofty spirits on the earth, on whom they lavished scientific knowledge. This science, however, belonged to institutes, authority, the laws; it was demanded and invoked by the elect but enjoyed the unconditional approval of the majority.

The music of the Sirens lies in another dimension entirely. It is the music of the cosmos, ordered and harmonic by definition. Music of movement and music to form movement, according to the Platonic concept, situated somewhere between primordial sound and the appearance of culture, part of a reverberating system halfway between acoustics and art, the physical phenomenon of nature and sonorous language become thought. Man, by exorcising the Sirens, deprived himself of this dimension. He canceled their every trace and preferred to inscribe on stone a hymn to Apollo, which is one of the earliest examples of official Western music. Thus the third-century Greek scholar Athenaeus could affirm:

> The knowledge of the ancient Greeks was prevalently related to music. They consequently held that the most musical and therefore most knowledgeable of the gods was Apollo, and of the demigods Orpheus.

Orpheus, the son of a Muse and a mortal—although some considered him actually to be the son of Apollo—achieved the rank of demigod not by birth but through merit; that is, through the intercession of Pluto and Persephone. A great manipulator of the elements and of consciousness through his music, Orpheus moves the rocks forming the walls, loosens plants from their roots, charms wild beasts, calms the winds, changes the courses of rivers, and opens the portals of Hades to return to the world of the living. However, Orpheus—literally, the solitary and obscure—is also a faithful votary of Apollo and therefore suppresses the song of the Sirens. Through the *Orphic Argonautica,* a work

The Muses defeat the Sirens and pluck out their feathers; drawing from the sarcophagus of the Odam family of Florence.

of the Byzantine era, we learn that what struck the Sirens dumb was an ode to events of violence, danger, war, and destruction.

Gold motivates the Argonauts in their enterprise, which was masculine as were few others. The Sirens imply the opposite choice. And in the final analysis, when Orpheus assails them with his music, he is doing battle for gold, to defend what has been won, or to merit the prize, as Seneca (4 B.C.?–A.D. 65) writes in *Medea:*

> *And when the horrible monsters*
> *with harmonious voice*
> *enchanted the waves of Ausonia*
> *the sound of Orpheus the Thracian's lyre*
> *almost forced the Sirens who beckon ships*
> *to follow that sound.*
> *And, as prize for this bold voyage:*
> *the golden fleece and Medea*
> *worse than the calamitous seas,*
> *just reward for the first ship.*

Much significant information has come down to us on this Thracian musician. For example, when Orpheus returned to the earth without Eurydice, he became misogynistic to the point of abandoning himself to unnatural gratifications, which explains why the women of Thrace fell upon him, tearing him to pieces. Some maintain that it was the Maenads, followers of Dionysus, who killed him in their fury because, as a player of the lyre, he was allied with Apollo. Plato confirms that Orpheus despised the feminine. Er was said to have seen the soul of Orpheus prefer the life of a swan; such was his hatred for the women who had murdered him that his soul would not be born from a woman's womb again.

His apotheosis awaited him. Although beset by the Maenads and made a victim of Dionysiac death, paralyzed and dismembered into a thousand fragments, Orpheus continued to act against silence. From the river Ebro, the sea current transported his lyre to Lesbos, where it was

Brooch of mother-of-pearl, ca. 1950.
From the author's collection.

kept as a holy relic in the temple. His head, which for a time emitted prophecies until Apollo himself destroyed it, was kept in a temple to Dionysus in a sea cave. His instrument ultimately ascended to the heavens to form the constellation Lyra, where it continues to watch over us.

As Apollonius, the most ancient of chroniclers, informs us, it was the stentorian nature of Orpheus's music that suffocated the voices of the Sirens. Orpheus, the great persuader, ceased to be persuasive before the Sirens and resorted to force. This is representative of a crucial change that occurred in Greek mythology. The aquatic principle was subjected to the terrestrial one. Heracles, the modern hero, routed Nereus, Triton, and Achelous. The Muses of Mount Helicon routed the Sirens.

Charles Picard, when observing the dispute depicted in classical art, rightly comments:

> It would be absolutely absurd to deny the historical echoes in the representations; they express the defeat of the power born of the sea, to the advantage of the new heroes favoured by the Ariani, enemies of the waves.

At the same time, the male aspect pushed aside the female one, attaching negative significance to it, vilifying it. Thus, in the *Odyssey,* Scylla is transformed from a woman into a horrible monster. Thus, the Erinys, or Furies, cease to act as such, are euphemized and rechristened Eumenides, and absolve the matricide of Orestes. And thus are the Muses invoked as initiators of life and the Sirens avoided as dispensers of death.

In Bachofen's thesis, endorsed by Engels, a matriarchal, Demeter-oriented phase in society, tied to telluric, pacific, and egalitarian laws, precedes the formation of the state, in which the new patriarchal laws of Apollo and Athena operate instead. In this context we can understand the defeat of the Sirens, daughters of Achelous, an old, vanquished water god, and of various mothers, who no longer had any importance.

The triumph of Orpheus over the Sirens represents the triumph of the instrument over the voice and of sonorous power over the secret

Marie Briot, the Sirens tempt the Argonauts; seventeenth-century woodcut in Baudoin's *Emblems*.

Bette Midler in *Divine Madness,* 1980. Courtesy of the archives of M. Gustin.

message. To no lesser degree, it represents the victory of the written word over the oral. In fact, Orphic knowledge is not transmitted by music but through "sacred texts" of which Plato speaks: Orphic tablets found on Greek, Cretan, and Roman tombs, which vaunt the celestial nature of the deceased. It should come as no surprise then that Orpheus is credited with the invention of the alphabet.

Voice of nature resounding with vital human rhythms, the music of the Sirens is so elusive as to resemble nothing. A music in tune with the aquatic and obscure feminine, it demands so active and subjective an attention as to go beyond the perceptive faculties of the senses, to involve risk.

Beginning with Orpheus, another musical tendency prevailed, one with a capacity to regulate, to order, which dominated and tended to produce and reproduce. This tendency constructed the walls of Thebes, placing stone upon stone to the rhythm of the lyre of Amphion. Or, inversely, it caused the walls of Jericho to fall before the trumpets of Joshua. Lyre and trumpet. This power no longer acts directly but only through the mediation of instruments, objects. The voice, however, which was defeated, persuades, attempts, promises, insinuates, seduces. *Seduce* meaning to conduct to oneself, to lead elsewhere, to divert, lead astray; to deviate, change course, shift, stray—actions that all belong to the secret and the ritual, given that what seduces is not obvious but hidden. Of the seductresses of the sea it has been said that they trained man in dying; which may also be true in the sense intended by Baudrillard in *Seduction:*

> Every male power is power of production. The feminine power is that of seduction. . . . It is a power of attraction and distraction, of absorption and fascination, a power that causes the collapse of not just sex, but the real in general—a power of defiance. It is never an economy of sex or speech, but an escalation of violence and grace, an instantaneous passion that can result in sex, but which can just as easily exhaust itself in the process of defiance and death. . . . Production, like revolution, puts an end to the epidemic of appearances. But seduction is inevitable. No one living escapes it—not even the dead. . . . Only those who do not wish to seduce or be seduced are dead. Seduction is part of a culture of cruelty, it is the only ceremonial form of it we have left.

If we accept this dimension, the wings of the Sirens could serve as the ornamental plumage, the showy finery of an extremely elaborate animal "courtship," a royal mantle, solemn fittings, vestments for the ceremony of total seduction.

Etymology, Number, Proper Names

On a painted Attic-Corinthian vase in the Louvre, found in Caere in Etruria from a period slightly later than the *Odyssey,* appears the figure of a cormorant with the face of a woman. Under the left wing is written "I am the Siren" in Greek.

Like almost all knowledge regarding the Sirens, the etymology of the word is uncertain. Does it come from the older Greek *seirios,* meaning either "incandescent" or "liable to deteriorate"? Or from *seraphin,* "to burn"? Or else from the Sanskrit *surya,* "sun" or "burning, unbearable drought"? If so, the reference is to the sun at its zenith, midday—the hour at which the Sirens act.

Another possibility is that the word comes from Sirius, the Dog Star, the most brilliant in the constellation Canis Major, because the star rules over the dog days. Or perhaps, since that star is almost always low on the horizon, it is associated with the realm of the hereafter. Sirius was the dwelling place of perfect souls, like the sun and the other fixed stars.

Aristotle listed, among the effects of the dog days on animals, hydrophobia in dogs and great agitation in the creatures of the sea. Furthermore, in situating the Sirens under the astronomical aegis of Sirius, their correlation with sacred aromas becomes evident, for myrrh and incense were cut for the harvest at the culminating phase of Sirius. And finally, siriasis, also known as sunstroke, has symptoms analogous to those of the dog days—prostration, drowsiness, apathy, cardiorespiratory insufficiency—like the hypnotic and fatal effects of the song of the Sirens.

Then again, could the term be derived from the Greek *seira:* snare, noose, cord, rope, belt. Or *seirazein,* "to bind," in the sense that the Sirens bound mariners to them, as these in turn bound their vessels to

"I am the Siren," painted on an Attic-Corinthian vase; Etruria, ca. 550 B.C. Louvre, Paris.

the land? Or could it be related to the other meaning of *seirazein,* which is "to drain" or "to dry up," particularly in reference to pastures?

The Copts had a similar word, *bra,* "to designate voice." The Semitic *sir* means "spell, magical chant"; St. Paul uses the term to refer to the chant of the synagogue, as effective as hymns in propagating the faith and quite different from *mizmor,* the simple psalmody. Latin and the Romance languages call the Sirens *Sirene,* which more closely assimilates them to *serenus,* the dry, cloudless, clear stretch of sky, mirroring the calm sea where they appear.

Every etymon here proposed confirms the prerogatives of the Sirens. They are an influence seemingly under the sway of magnetism, gravitational force—the action of attracting to oneself, dragging, turning away, distracting, and averting. Rendering serene, sidereal, benumbed. Bind, fasten, tighten, allure, lure, ensnare, encircle, wrap, clasp, clutch, cling, fascinate, attract, charm. Sirens do not vanquish, they enthrall. The word designating them has a phonic value of its own, a resounding, sweet, murmuring singsong, serene as the stilled sea that presages their appearance, the waves flat as a terminated electroencephalogram, serene as death.

The number of the Sirens is eight. It is also the number of Demeter and Poseidon. Eight is associated with the eight spheres of ancient astronomy, with the musical octave, the first cubic number $(2 \times 2 \times 2)$, and the eight directions of the winds. In astrology, the house of death is denominated by eight. For Christianity, eight is the number of beatitudes, the emblem of regeneration for St. Ambrose, and of resurrection for St. Augustine. Carrying this random association to its extreme, eight is the atomic number of oxygen, an essential component of air and water, and an element indispensable to every vital process. Venturing even further, in modern mathematics, a number eight placed horizontally is the graphic symbol for infinity.

Furthermore, the Sirens' classical names number eight and echo the qualities of their voices. Beside a red figure of a Siren on a vase from Vulci we find the most ancient of those names: Himeropa ("voice that

Label of an eau de cologne from Capri.

ARIA DI CAPRI

EAU DE TOILETTE

provokes desire"), subsequently transformed into Eumolpe ("she who sings well") and Moeolpe ("the harmonious").

Scholars of Homer specify a triad: Aglaope or Aglaophonos ("of the shrill voice"), Theixiope ("she of the song that alleviates, soothes"), sometimes called Thelxione, and Pisinoe also known as Persinoe, Peisinue, Pasinoe ("the persuasive"). The latter is replaced by the editors of Apollonius of Rhodes with Moeolpe, and often another name is added, Cyane ("the blue").

The most famous name, venerated in Magna Grecia and later on a recurrent reference for the humanists, is that of Leucosia or Leucothea ("the white goddess"), Ligea or Ligheia or Ligi ("the clear voice"), and Parthenope ("the virgin").

As regards place, Homer assigns them Anthemoessa, a flower-covered island not far from the Strait of Messina, since Ulysses' enterprise, immediately following his encounter with the Sirens, was the attempt to pass unscathed between the shoals of Scylla and Charybdis. Lycophron (third century B.C.) informs us that the Sirens were born in the vicinity of Etna, which would link them to the chthonian, terrestrial forces, and that after the kidnapping of Persephone they fled toward the sea to Cape Pelorus. Strabo (63 B.C.–A.D. 25), in his *Geography,* situates them in two places: on the Sicilian coast and on the promontory of Sorrento, between the Gulf of Naples and Posidonia. Still other authors indicate as their earlier home the Sirenuse, small islands today called Li Galli, which can be seen to the south of the Sorrento peninsula. However, it is most widely believed that the home of the Sirens is the island of Capri, at once rocky and flower covered, where there is even a rock in Marina Piccola named after them.

Many hold that, after the defeat dealt them by Ulysses, the Sirens threw themselves into the sea, intent on committing suicide, and that the bodies of the three most dear were deposited by the waves on the coast of Campania. The Tre Pizzi ("Three Points") at the end of Marina del Cantone, off the Amalfi coast, are said to be their mutation into stone.

Leucosia is said by some to have ended up on the coast of a small island in the Tyrrhenian Sea that would take her name. Others think she stopped south of Paestum, at Licosia, or on the hill of Enipeus, finding her final burial place on Cape Posidonia.

Ligea, torn to pieces by a sea monster, would be carried by the currents as far as Terina (today Santa Eufemia). There, on the sandy shore, sailors prepared her body for eternity.

The lifeless body of Parthenope was washed ashore at the foot of the tower of Phalera, where the inhabitants built a tomb that became an object of veneration, with yearly libations and hecatombs. In her honor, the city took the name of Parthenope. When it was later destroyed by the Cumaeans, upon the sepulchre of the Siren, which remained intact, a new city (Neapolis, later Naples) was built. But the cult of Parthenope, who was honored together with Demeter, fell into oblivion. In a brief attempt at restoration by the Athenian navarch Diotimus, the cities of Parthenope and Terina minted coins on which the Sirens were depicted. But, of this as well, there is little memory.

1
Classic Sirens

Pagan and Christian, Siren and Angel

Cicero (106–43 B.C.) maintained that the Sirens—like the serpent in the Garden of Eden—tempted men with knowledge. Observing children and adult spectators at the circus—made oblivious of their hunger and thirst by the curiosity of what was before them—he deduced that the love of knowledge for its own sake was innate in human nature.

Virgil (70–19 B.C.) considered the existence of Sirens a foregone conclusion. In the *Aeneid,* Poseidon and his court, the Tritons, the host of Phorcus, and the Nereids in the retinue of Tethys still flourish. But the desolation of the places once inhabited by the Sirens speaks eloquently of their absence. The voyage of Aeneas proceeds through the newly emerged signs of death: the pyre on the shore is a reminder of Dido's suicide, and of Palinurus, sacrificial victim to the sea god, who, overcome by fatigue, fell asleep at the helm and was lost into the sea.

Although Pliny the Elder (A.D. 23–79) was not convinced that bird-women existed, in his *Historia Naturalis* he speculates on a variety of other "things so monstrous as to be incredible": the color of the Abyssinians, the stature of the Pygmies, the white hair of the albino, and the cannibalism of the Scythians; the hermaphrodites whom "Aristotle described as having one male breast on the right and one female one on the left"; creatures on Mount Milo with eight toes on each foot who walk backward; people who hop about rapidly on their only foot, which

Rene Magritte, *The Collective Invention*, 1949.
© 1998 C. Herscovici, Brussels/Artists Rights Society, New York.

is also useful for making shade when they rest; others who copulate with wild beasts, generating mixed breeds such as the satyr and the cynocephalus. On the Sirens, Pliny was more circumspect:

> Nor yet do the Sirens obtain any greater credit with me, although Dinon, the father of Clearchus, a celebrated writer, asserts that they exist in India, and that they charm men by their song, and, having first lulled them to sleep, tear them to pieces. The person, however, who may think fit to believe in these tales, may probably not refuse to believe also that dragons licked the ears of Melampodes, and bestowed upon him the power of understanding the language of birds.

In concise verses, Martial (A.D. 40–103) expresses the ambivalent effect Sirens have on man: "The hilarious pain of the seamen / soft death, cruel pleasure." Claudianus (A.D. 370?–404), too, points out the extreme, and apparently conflicting, sentiments they inspire:

> Sirens, sweet fruit of the sea, bird-maidens, lived among the waves of Scylla and Charybis. Their sacred music, gentle danger of the sea, was pleasurable terror among the waves. On the keel of the ship lingered the caressing air, while from aft, a voice invaded the ship. But the seaman longed not to take the secure route home. But there was no pain; joy itself dealt death.

Reflecting on Plato's allegory of the afterlife, Plutarch offers a deeply religious interpretation:

> The song of the Siren, far from being inhuman and murderous, inspires in the souls emigrating from the earth to the underworld, errant after death, oblivion for that which is transient and a love for that which is divine. And the souls, captivated by the harmony of their song, follow it and bind themselves to it.

Various authors attest to the vogue enjoyed by the Sirens during the reign of Hadrian (A.D. 117–138). While they were apparently sighted by Dionysius the Areopagite at Sorrento, others attribute to them a purely metaphorical significance. The Sirens find a specific place in the Bestiaries, beginning with the *Physiologous,* an Alexandrian volume of the second century that is a mixture of Gnostic, Hermetic, and Hebrew cultures and along with the Bible was the most consulted text during the Middle Ages:

> Physiologous said that in the sea there exist animals called Sirens, who are not unlike the Muses in that they sing harmoniously, and that when passing sailors hear their song they dive into the sea and perish. They are half human and half goose. . . . Some men, when in church, can appear normal, but once distant change into beasts, like the Sirens, who deceive Godfearing men with their sweet, seductive speech.

The Sirens became the negative in comparisons, used to impart a moral lesson. In the *Physiologous* that lesson is made more convincing with passages from the Letters to the Romans and the Corinthians, in which Paul warns of the perfidy of seductive speech.

Images succeed where words fail. An illustration in the *Brussels Manuscript,* a later version of the *Physiologous,* shows two Sirens bestially lacerating the flesh of a man. In early Christian art and in the allegories of patristic philosophy, they are associated with evil, personifying all opinions contrary to those of the church: the pleasures of the senses, diabolic temptation. Some are represented with the papyrus scroll of the scholar and the orator's mantle; however, the feathers they wear on their heads, an attribute no longer theirs but the Muses', demonstrate the hypocrisy of their culture.

Ulysses' resistance to the Sirens is usually exalted, offered as an edifying example. The same is true of Orpheus. One of the first images of Christ, from the third century, portrayed him together with the Thracian musician, who had been elevated by the apologists as his prophet, identifying him with the Good Shepherd, he who guides the flock with

Two sirens tear a man to pieces while a third plays the lute;
fourteenth century, *Brussels Manuscript.*

his Word. A phrase from Clement of Alexandria will serve to illuminate these interpretations: "Those who were as if dead and did not partake of the true life were revived by the sound of their song."

The Sirens remain those who deviate or lead astray, and therefore must be firmly rejected by man, as they would distract him from the path of righteousness and truth. While they offer pleasure and science, it is erotic pleasure and pagan science, and consequently to be rejected. Thus, the only bird with positive connotations left in the skies above the ships was the dove, the manifestation of the Holy Spirit and often of the souls of the faithful, bearing the grape and the golden bough, participating in the triumph of Christ. Of winged hybrids there remained only the safe angels as a substitute for ambiguous Sirens, with whom they would no longer be confused, even morphologically. The title of winged messengers from the otherworld would be exclusively theirs—the Accadian cherubim who during the Exodus covered the holy Ark of the Covenant with their wings and the Hebrew seraphim seen by Isaiah "standing above the Lord," each with three pairs of wings with which to fly and to cover their faces and feet.

The same root as that of enflame, burn, illuminate, unites the words *seraphim* and *Siren*. But the Sirens no longer illuminated or enlightened. The favors all went to the angels. Even music—august and revealing music—became theirs. The intermediaries between audible human music and inaudible celestial music were the musician angels, and comprehension of divine truth came through the psalm. Univocal, the singing of the angels expressed all-embracing consensus, the hymn in praise of creation, the only song which could be called sublime.

A numerical relation continued to exist, although the ruling number had become three. Beginning with the Apocalyptic visions of the seven trumpet-bearing angels, Dionysius the Aeropagite—the Athenian converted to Christianity by Paul—defines the three choirs of celestial hierarchies within which the angels are ranged according to their degree of light and proximity to God. The first is reserved for the seraphim, cherubim, and thrones; the second to dominations, virtues, and powers; and the third to principalities, archangels, and angels. Hierarchy, rank, and subordination are nonexistent for the Sirens as presented by Homer or Plato. Indeed, Plato himself became a "Siren," and with him all pre-Christian philosophical thought, in that it represents eloquent rhetoric, which ensnares and menaces eternal salvation.

For Clement of Alexandria, Ulysses bound to the ship's mast was comparable to Christ on the cross. His successor, Hippolytus, professed the same opinion and recommended stopping up the ears against gnosis, the threat to common mortals. Methodius of Olympus did not refer to the cross but suggested that the voices of the prophets and the Apostles act as a shield against the mortal song of the Sirens.

One hundred years later Ambrose of Milan (340–397), although providing an introspective interpretation, identified the Sirens with sensual pleasures and the cliffs with the temptations of the flesh. At the same time he preached that one should listen only to the words of Christ and bind oneself to the mast of the cross. Reinforcing this, Ambrose cites a famous passage from the Old Testament in which Jeremiah claims that the abode of the daughters of the Sirens is Babylon, comparing the enticements and worldly confusion of that city to those mythical symbols of lasciviousness.

In translating the Bible into Greek, in the passage where Micah refers to the doleful song heard on the invasion of Judaea as "ostriches bursting into lamentations," the Septuagint substituted "Sirens" for "ostriches." Evidently, in the choice of terms, the classical idea of the mournful Siren prevailed. Seven centuries later, while composing the Vulgate, Jerome (347–420) also translated the Hebrew word *tannim* (jackals) as "Sirens," in the passages in which Isaiah announces that the inhabitants of the immoral and corrupt Babylon would be driven out by the desert fauna. To one of them Jerome adds the annotation: ". . . et sirenes in delubris voluptatis."

An observation made by Cerquand is interesting in this light. He believes that the Greeks of Syria and Egypt likened their deserts to the sea: the same solitude, the same dangers. However, the Bible contained neither Sirens nor the demonology of the Kabbalah. The only fabulous sea creatures mentioned by Jehovah as a sign of his own omnipotence, at

Lilith, terra-cotta bas-relief,
Sumeria, ninth-century B.C.
Collection of Norman Colville.

the end of his lecture to Job, were Behemoth and Leviathan, identified respectively with the hippopotamus and the crocodile. Only Lilith, the dark Mesopotamian mother figure, mentioned by Isaiah in that same passage, might have some characteristics in common with the Sirens, although the association with water is absent in her. Traditionally, Lilith is an attractive, long-haired woman with wings and claws who arouses man's lust. These are perhaps the underlying motifs emerging from translations of both the Septuagint and Jerome, which opened the way to a rich vein of negative associations with the Sirens. That fate, of course, was not exclusively reserved to them but to women in general, under the influence of the new ascetic and misogynist currents of thought: Pythagoreanism, Orphism, and Christianity.

For Augustine (350–430), the Sirens were the symbol of rhetoric: they had lured him and almost succeeded in leading him away from the road to salvation; that is, from philosophy and faith. Although the fourth-century Virgilian scholar Servius provided some information on the music of the Sirens, he banalized them, reducing them to the level of prostitutes out to ruin men.

> The Sirens as the fables recount are three, part woman and part bird, daughters of the river Achelous and the Muse Calliope. One sings, the other plays the flute, and the third the lyre. They lived initially near to Peloro and later on the island of Capri.... They caused shipwrecks, attracting men with their song. In truth, they were strumpets who reduced those who passed to poverty.

Maximus, Bishop of Turin from 466 to 470, in one of his sermons exhausted the allegorical repertoire of Christianity: the sea corresponds to a hostile world, the Sirens to pernicious pleasure; Ithaca to the celestial realm; the ship to the church guided by Christ; the mast to the cross, Ulysses to the human condition, the sailors his companions to the good thief with Christ, and even the wax placed in their ears is compared to the sacred scriptures.

Isidor of Seville (540–636), echoing the commentary of Servius, simply skipped over geographic collocation. However, the knowledgeable author of the *Etymologies* did add that the Sirens had wings and claws, offering an explanation: love is capable of flight and of wounding, and they inhabit the waves because the sea created Venus.

In a somewhat simplistic way, a new quality was attributed to the Sirens, eventually becoming their distinguishing characteristic: eroticism. All their spiritual qualities having been passed on to the angels who, being immaterial and possessing a nature similar to the soul, were sexless, the Sirens became the agents of perdition through sex, and the bearers of eternal death.

In the *De Naturis Animalium* written at the beginning of the second millennium by Theobald, Abbot of Monte Cassino, we read that the Sirens are sea monsters capable of music that attracts and distracts the mariner. Their concerts of dulcet voices cause disaster and mortal danger.

David Delamare, *The Call of the Sirens*, 1982. © 1994 David Delamare, Portland, Oregon.

Those who escape their wiles describe them as beautiful virgins down to the navel but with monstrous lower bodies in the form of birds.

Conceptions prefiguring humanism alternated with others purely devotional and moralistic. In the twelfth century the most important commentators on Sirens were Honoré d'Autun, the Alsatian monk Herrad of Landsberg, and Eustathius, Bishop of Thessalonica and scholar of Homer.

Honoré, in order to propagate the faith, presented to his flock his revised version of the ancient pagan myth in which Ulysses became a duke. The Sirens were presented as mystic images despite the fact that they were invented by the enemies of Christ. The sea signified the terrestrial sphere perpetually prey to tempests of affliction. Their island was the image of worldly joys, and the three Sirens who with their pleasant song seduced seafarers, sending them into an eternal sleep, were the three concupiscences who render men vulnerable.

One of the clearest examples of Christian iconography and symbolism was offered by Herrad of Landsberg (1130?–1195) in his *Hortus Deliciarum,* an anthology composed for Pope Honorius III for the instruction of novices in the Monastery of Saint Odile. The original manuscript, which contained poetry, miniatures, and music, some produced by Herrad himself, was almost destroyed in a fire in the Library of Strasbourg. From what was saved, we learn that the Sirens, "lusting passions who at times use nets to draw in their victims," are the dangers that Christ must overcome in order to lead his church. Tall and slim with tapering hands, large wings, and long tunics, the Sirens of Herrad would seem to be saints of the epoch were it not for their birds' claws. On the waves, one sings, another plays the transverse flute, yet another the psaltery as the sailors fall into a trance. A second vignette illustrates the subsequent phase: having boarded the ship, the Sirens proceed to tear their victims apart; visible in a transparent sea is a drowned sailor. However, it is only a nightmare or an admonition. In fact, if one is to be saved, explains the text, the strategy of Ulysses must be adopted, and the following conclusion is clearly allegorical: "And thus he escapes the danger unscathed, pushing the Sirens back to the bottom of the sea." The phrase, however, is illustrated literally in the third vignette, which shows the Sirens being killed by the sailors: one is being bent double, her claws still dug into the helm, another is dragged down by her hair, and the third is pushed with a long pole, lifeless, under the waves.

In his commentary on Homer's work, Eustathius stressed the parallelisms, and in doing so proposed once more the didactic concepts of the ancient Greeks. Ulysses became the master, and as he was learned, he

Drawings from the *Hortus Deliciarum* by Herrad of Landsberg, ca. 1170.

was allowed to express himself in the first person, and over his disciples he had the power of choice, censorship, and prohibition. Thus he stopped up their ears with wax, the meaning of which is a solid and firm instruction. He who is wise can—in fact, must—have the experience, however, with the proper precautions: the ropes, in fact, belong to philosophy. The mast mirrors the erect and irreproachable attitude of the master.

The medieval bestiaries, whose prototype was the *Physiologous*, fused the information from that source with that from the apologists, opening the way to the first encyclopedic lucubrations. Two schools of thought resulted: one from Isaiah/*Physiologous* and the other from Servius/Isidor. To the first belonged *The Cambridge Bestiary*, written in Latin in the twelfth century, which declared that Sirens are mortally

Hieronimus Bosch, *The Garden of Earthly Delight;* detail from the central panel of the tryptic, fifteenth century. Prado Museum, Madrid.

dangerous creatures with a human head and a human torso and the extremities of a bird. They sing melodious songs in a voice that caresses the ears of distant mariners. Their song calms and seduces men, causing them to fall into a profound torpor, after which the Sirens fall upon them and tear their bodies to pieces.

> Those who spend their lives in the pursuit of the pleasures of the flesh and the delights of wealth, dissolute and corrupt and lulled by the music of feasts and spectacles, inevitably losing lucidity and mental vigour and falling prey to their enemies, must inevitably die.

The *Bestiaire* of Pierre le Picard, produced between the twelfth and thirteenth centuries, reemphasized the lethargic effect of the song of the Sirens and the murder of seamen in their sleep, concluding as follows:

> The Sirens represent the mad women who attract men and lead them to poverty and death with the softness and the deceit of their words. The wings of the Sirens are a woman's love which, inconstant, comes and goes.

Jacques de Vitry, in his *Orientalis Sive Hierosolymitana Historia,* written before 1240, attempted to classify Sirens zoologically:

> The Sirens resemble virgins down to their navels, while their lower parts have the appearance of birds; thus, they are considered seabirds, despite their exceptional nature.

For Dante (1265–1321) Paradise was a geometrical structure that recalled that of Plato, where motion, music, and light were in harmony. The poet referred to the Sirens, together with the Muses, to describe the superior quality of the song intoned by the luminous spirits of the eight heavens.

Dante, who was familiar only indirectly with Homer, was not par-

ticularly fond of Ulysses, whom he has burn in the inferno together with
Diomedes for the crime of political fraud. For those other bird-women,
the Harpies, he reserved an extreme punishment: damned to the seventh
circle, nesting on forbidding brambles, tormenting the souls of suicides.
Yet far from demonizing the Sirens, as most authors of that time were
wont to do, Dante placed them in purgatory. Judging from the words
he gives a Siren, he might have confused her with Circe. And at that
moment just before dawn, when the constellation of Pisces is high in the
heavens, the poet, on the point of joining the circle of the incontinents,
transfigures every unpleasantness.

> *There came to me in my dream a babbling woman*
> *cross-eyed, club footed*
> *handless, pallid face.*
> *"I am," she sang, "I am sweet siren*
> *who leads astray mariners at sea*
> *full of pleasure to be heard!*
> *I turned Ulysses from his vague journey*
> *to my chant; and who ever listens to me,*
> *rarely leaves; so I do satisfy, quench his thirst!"*

In "Sonnet 167," Petrarch (1304–1374) sees in Laura a Siren whose
troubling voice leads him to a change so unusual as to convince him that
he is at the point of death.

> *When Love casts her eyes downward*
> *and all her emotions she gathers in a sigh*
> *with her hands, and releases them in her voice*
> *clear, soft, angelic, divine,*
>
> *I feel my heart become sweet prey*
> *so deeply changed my thoughts and wishes*
> *that I say: Take my last remains*
> *if Heaven decrees me a death so honest.*

But the sound that binds sweetness to my senses
wishing to be blessed by hearing
the soul, ready to leave, halts.

That she makes me live, that she spins, lets out
the twine of life that is given to me,
this lone siren from Heaven among us.

Renaissance Sirens

With wood engravings and the invention of the printing press, the master-pieces of literature and ancient art began to diffuse. Consequently, the sea enchantresses too began to break out of their medieval crystallizations.

Angelo Poliziano (1454–1494) compared the fluid chant of the Sirens to the ardent song of his beloved Ipolita, equally dangerous, but possessing the power to heal.

They with their song, the Sirens
In the sea would lead the mariner to drown:
But Ipolita mine singing keeps
Always in the fire her poor lovers,
Only one remedy is there for my suffering,
That once more Ipolita sing
And with the song which has wounded me heal me,
With the song that killed me revive me.

Erasmus of Rotterdam (1466–1536), in his *Manual of the Christian Soldier,* offered ethical advice, tinged with humanist overtones, saying that during his military life, a young man must study the works of the pagan poets and philosophers, but he must do so without lingering on the cliffs of the Sirens. The illustrations of the period amply reveal the hidden and disturbing aspect of the feminine. The Sirens, dispensers of death, appear to belong to the realm of the bruised, the swollen, the tumified, the putrid, so that the reader's fantasies and hallucinations can be remolded around them.

Aubrey Beardsley, illustration for
Le Morte d'Arthur by Thomas Malory, 1893.

In the *Arcades,* the visions of John Milton (1608–1674) converge
with those of Pythagoras and Plato: the Sirens sing from the adamantine
spheres in the midst of the night, when sleep has rendered insignificant
any morality. And in *Comus,* considered the best of Milton's early works,
Sirens rush to save Lady Alice, held prisoner by the magician Comus,
who speaks:

> *My Mother Circe with the Sirens three,*
> *Amidst the flowery-kirtled Naiades,*
> *Culling their potent herbs, and baleful drugs,*
> *Who as they sung, would take the prisoned soul,*
> *And lap it in Elysium, Scylla wept,*
> *And chid her barking waves into attention,*
> *And fell Charybdis murmured soft applause:*
> *Yet they in pleasing slumber lulled the sense,*
> *And in sweet madness robbed it of itself;*
> *But such a sacred, and home-felt delight,*
> *Such sober certainty of waking bliss*
> *I never heard till now. I'll speak to her*

And she shall be my Queen. Hail foreign wonder
Whom certain these rough shades did never breed.

Calderón de la Barca (1600–1681) provides us with a piscatory eulogy, entitled *El golfo de las Sirenas,* for which he availed himself of the extremely elaborate scenic staging of the Florentine engineer Cosimo Lotti. The action takes place in Trinacria (Sicily). Ulysses is tempted on a number of occasions by Scylla, the huntress, and by Charybdis, the Siren, as he attempts to decide which of the two senses, sight or hearing, is the most important, or rather, which beauty lends itself more to seduction: that of the body or that of the voice?

> ULYSSES: Which of the two shall I follow?
>   I know not (alas), I know not,
>   For the metal of my senses
>   is attracted with equal force
>   by the north of that which they hear
>   and the magnet of what they see. . . .
> CHARYBDIS: To look but not see,
> ULYSSES: Between looking and seeing,
>   what distinction can there be?
> CHARYBDIS: Looking at beauty is looking,
>   And seeing the danger is seeing.
> SCYLLA: Although hearing is not listening.
> ULYSSES: What distinction do you make between
>   hearing and listening, to separate them thus?
> SCYLLA: Hearing is only hearing
>   and listening actively attentive. . . .
> ULYSSES: The steps hesitate,
>   Sweet enchantment; for follow you
>   in fact I shall. Impossible,
>   being one, to follow both.
>
> THE TWO (from within): So, we shall say all three. . . .

THE THREE: For between sight and hearing
  the advantage is that something always
  remains to be heard, but not to be seen. . . .

CHORUS OF SIRENS: Who from the Earth flees
  after having seen and heard pleasure and pain,
  and seeing and hearing the sea
  feels, cries, cries and suffers
  knowing that the waters of the Gulf of the Sirens
  once ploughed, plough him with sadness.

The Sirens during the Classical and Romantic Periods

In Germanic literature the winged feminine figures most often encountered are not the Sirens but the Valkyries, who can transform themselves

Ivan Bilibine, illustration on the cover of a book of stories.
From the archives of Paola Pallottino.

into swans with a magic ring or, with the aid of feathered tunics, fly over the fields of battle. Their very name (from *valr,* "fallen in battle," and *kyria,* "she who chooses") implies their function, similar to that of the Alexandrian Sirens—to care for the souls of heroes who have fallen in battle, accompanying them—in this case—to the paradise of Valhalla.

Johann Wolfgang Goethe (1749–1832), an Olympian classicist, declared: "It is wonderful to be a Homeride, even the last of them." In the second part of *Faust,* he gave ample space to the ancient Sirens but without associating them with the protagonist's insatiable thirst for knowledge. Charged with alchemical symbolism, they are present at the fundamental passage of man—and metal—from base to noble. When Faust evokes Helen, beckoning her to rise from the realm of the dead, through a classical Walpurgis Night in which Greek reason, elementary forces, and demons all appear, Sirens enter more than once: on the banks of the Peneus and in the rocky bays of the Aegean Sea, together with the Sphinx, the Hydra of Lerna, the centaur Chiron, giant ants, griffins, Pygmies, lamiae, oreads, and dryads.

> *When Ulysses passed among us*
> *he found nothing of which to disapprove,*
> *but many tales to tell!*
> *To you we wish to confide all these*
> *if you wish to live in those places*
> *with us on the azure sea.*

Ancient beauty, felt intensely, would shape the poetry of John Keats (1795–1821). We can easily imagine him in ecstasy before the marbles of the Parthenon newly arrived at the British Museum, as he exclaims: "Being mortal oppresses me like troubled sleep." A brief mention of the Sirens is had in "Endymion":

> *Fair melody!*
> *Kind Syren!*
> *I've no choice.*

As Keats stated in a letter, a passage from *King Lear*—"Do you not hear the sea?"—had been the obsession of his sleepless nights: he desired to close his eyes and be awakened by a chorus of Sirens. In "On Sitting Down to Read *King Lear* Once Again," there is another well-known reference:

> *O golden-tongued Romance with serene lute!*
> *Fair plumed syren! Queen of far-away!*
> *Leave melodizing on this wintry day,*
> *Shut up thine olden pages, and be mute:*
> *Adieu! for once again the fierce dispute*
> *Betwixt damnation and impassion'd clay*
> *Must I burn through; once more humbly assay*
> *The bitter-sweet of this Shakespearian fruit.*

The passion of the Romantic English writers for Italy is proverbial; Italy, realm of art and beauty as then unspoiled by the Industrial Revolution, chosen as the destination of their pilgrimages by Rogers, Murray,

Cesare Vincenzi, *Trio of Sirens*; woodcut.

Byron, Browning, Keats, and Shelley, who perished there. Before he carried off his wife, Elisabeth Barrett, on a prolonged Italian holiday, Robert Browning (1823–1899) described his astonished encounter with Campania in a long poem entitled *The Englishman in Italy, Piano di Sorrento.* The poet holds Fortù, the child of the South, on his knees, inviting her to explore the Island of the Sirens, at the time no more than three uninhabited rocky crags.

> *All is silent and grave—*
> *'Tis a sensual and timorous beauty—*
> *How fair, but a slave!*
> *So I turned to the sea,—and there slumbered*
> *As greenly as ever*
> *Those isles of the syren, your Galli;*
> *No ages can sever*
> *The Three—nor enable their sister*
> *To join them,—half way*
> *On the voyage, she looked at Ulysses—*
> *No farther to-day,*
> *Tho' the small one, just launched in the wave,*
> *Watches breast-high and steady*
> *From under the rock, her bold sister*
> *Swum half-way already.*
> *O when shall we sail there together*
> *And see from the sides*
> *Quite new rocks show their faces—new haunts*
> *Where the syren abides?*
> *Oh, to sail round and round them, close over*
> *The rocks, tho' unseen,*
> *That ruffle the grey glassy water*
> *To glorious green,—*
> *Then scramble from splinter to splinter,*
> *Reach land and explore*
> *On the largest, the strange square black turret*

With never a door—
Just a loop that admits the quick lizards;
—To stand there and hear
The birds' quiet singing, that tells us
What life is, so clear;
The secret they sang to Ulysses,
When ages ago
He heard and he knew this life's secret
I hear and I know!

Reappearances since the Late Nineteenth Century

Giovanni Pascoli (1855–1912), a learned scholar of classical literature, dedicated to the Sirens some of his most penetrating writing. Reflected in the mirror of water, they appear as a mirage to the aged Ulysses, at the moment of his final voyage. This time he is ready to plunge into the absolute, at last to know the ultimate truth.

And the old man saw that the two Sirens,
their brows raised,
looked before them, straight into the sun,
or him, or in his black ship.
And on the immobile calm of the sea,
he raised his voice, loud and strong.
"Here I am. Here I am! I have come back to know!
For I did see, just as you see me.
Only that everything I saw in the world
saw me and made me ask: 'Who am I?'"
And the rapid sweet current
urged the ship ever on.
And the old man saw a large pile of human bones
and withered skin around,
near the two Sirens, immobile
lying still on the beach, like two rocks.

"I see. So be it. These hard bones
will increase the pile. But, you two, speak to me!
But tell me the truth, one truth only among all
before I die, so I can say I have lived!"
And the rapid sweet current
urged the ship ever on.
And the two Sirens raised their gaze
to the ship eyes set.
"I have only an instant. I beg of you!
Tell me at least who I am. Who I was!"
And between the two rocks the ship crashed.

The Irishman William Butler Yeats (1865–1939) gave dramatic form to the cycle of Celtic legends of Ulster, composed between the seventh and eighth centuries. Against a timeless background, in a theatrical setting consisting of rocky reefs frequented only by seagulls and witches of the air, unfolds the passion, death, and rebirth of Cuchulain, who has unknowingly killed his own son. To atone for his heinous deed,

Ventura Rodriguez, *Fallen Angel*, 1878; Siren riding a gigantic lobster. Parque Retiro, Madrid. Photograph by Giovanni Longobardi.

he rushes against the sea with his sword, as in the final encounter with the enemy. A woman of Sidhe, the "Country-under-Wave," behaves like a Siren. With metal mask and long hair, she dances around Cuchulain. Emer, his wife, will leave him, so that he may save himself, but Cuchulain will betray her yet once more for his profane lover.

> EMER: Who is this woman?
> FIGURE OF CUCHULAIN: She has hurried from the
> Country-under-Wave
> And dreamed herself into that shape that he
> May glitter in her basket; for the Sidhe
> Are dexterous fishers and they fish for men
> With dreams upon the hook.

At the beginning of the twentieth century, as during the Romantic period, Italy had a strong attraction for Anglo-Saxon intellectuals who identified it with pagan sensuality and artistic freedom, comparing it to the Puritan England held up to scorn by Oscar Wilde. One of the most brilliant experts on things Italian was Norman Douglas (1868–1952), who, in 1911, published a book on the Sorrentine peninsula and Capri entitled *Siren Land*.

It was the Emperor Tiberius who startled his grammarians with the question, what songs the Sirens sang? I suspect he knew more about the matter than they did, for he was a Siren-worshipper all his life, though fate did not allow him to indulge his genius till those last few years which he spent among them on the rock-islet of Capri.

This is Siren Land. To the south lie the islets of the Sirens, nowadays known as the Galli; westwards, Capri, appropriately associated with them from its craggy and yet alluring aspect; Sorrento, whose name has been derived from them—I wonder some adventurous scholar has not identified it with the Homeric *Surie*—lies on the northern slope. A favoured land, flowing with milk and honey; particularly the former.

Thus does Douglas see the connection between these solar lands, the second Roman emperor, and the Sirens: a land of cults more pagan than Christian, where there is an affinity between meteorology and mind; an emperor who appreciated the vital sensation of plunging into the waters, and who faced death with an attitude of deep serenity; and finally, the Sirens, who offered men the precious gifts of leisure as opposed to diligence, and digression instead of the usual, beaten paths and convention.

Captivated by the ancient Sirens, Guillaume Apollinaire (1880–1918) makes recurring references to them in his poetry. In "Lul de Fantenin," a poem belonging to the collection *Alcools,* Apollinaire abandons himself to the ambivalence, placing the Sirens in an enigmatic register.

> *Sirens I crept toward your caverns*
> *You stuck your tongues out at the waves*
> *And danced before their horses*
> *Then clapped your angel wings*
> *While I listened to those rival choirs . . .*
>
> *If the boatmen have rowed off*
> *Far from the lips at water level*
> *Thousands upon thousands of charmed beasts*
> *Sniff out the trail leading*
> *To my beloved wounds.*
>
> *Their eyes bestial stars*
> *Illumine my compassion*
> *No matter my wisdom equals*
> *That of the constellations*
> *For it is I alone night that seeds you with stars*
>
> *At last sirens I descend*
> *Into a gaping cave I love*
> *Your eyes the steps are slippery*

Turning you into dwarves from afar
You no longer entice anybody.

Birds sticking your tongues out at the sea
Yesterday's sun caught up to me
Heraldic bars cover us with blood
In the nest of the sirens far
From the flocks of oblong stars

James Joyce's (1882–1941) *Ulysses* parallels the *Odyssey*, concentrating in a single summer's day of 1904 all the Odyssean adventures of a modern hero, Leopold Bloom, advertising agent. The sea in question is Dublin, with its ever-present crowds and unpredictable situations that follow one another in an uninterrupted flow. Episode XI, named after the Sirens, focuses on the sense of hearing. The form—according to the Gorman-Gilbert scheme approved by Joyce—would be a fugue for four voices, with eight themes and a "stretto" finale—a coincidence or a deliberate reference to the Pythagorean and Platonic numbers associated with the Sirens?

In the episode, Bloom has just taken leave of Bella Cohen (Circe), the mistress of the brothel, and heads for the Ormond Bar, where Miss Douce and Miss Kennedy serve the public. These two waitresses are the equivalent of the Homeric Sirens. The author describes them as "venereal," the first with bronze-colored hair and the second with golden hair, so vapid they might float away, derelicts of love and contaminated by smoke. Myriad acoustic stimuli envelops the protagonist: the pounding of horses' hooves, the ring of coins thrown onto the bar, the clock sounding the hour—four o'clock in the afternoon, another coincidence?—fragments of real music such as the tenor's aria from Flotow's *Martha*, which Stephen Dedalus (Telemachus) sings gaily. Sonorous images rush by: a thrush's song, a blackbird, snoring, a mournful whistle, a tuning fork, the sound of a piano from the room next door, violins, a cello, a harp. The phonic charge of words subtends the entire episode: the onomatopoeia, the approach of syllables, and the narrative language follow the flow of consciousness, protean as the sea itself.

Wise Bloom eyed on the door a poster, a swaying mermaid smoking mid nice waves. Smoke mermaids, coolest whiff of all. Hair streaming: lovelorn. . . .

From the saloon a call came, long in dying. That was a tuning-fork the tuner had that he forgot that he now struck. A call again. That he now poised that it now throbbed. You hear? It throbbed, pure, purer, softly and softlier, its buzzing prongs. Longer in dying call. . . .

A voiceless song sang from within, singing:

— . . . the morn is breaking.

A duodene of birdnotes chirruped bright treble answer under sensitive hands. Brightly the keys, all twinkling, linked, all harpsichording, called to a voice to sing the strain of dewy morn, of youth, of love's leavetaking, life's, love's morn. . . .

Down stage he strode some paces, grave, tall in affliction, his long arms outheld. Hoarsely the apple of his throat hoarsed softly. Softly he sang to a dusty seascape there: *A Last Farewell*. A headland, a ship, a sail upon the billows. Farewell. A lovely girl, her veil awave upon the wind upon the headland, wind around her.

Cowley sang:

—*M'appari tutt'amor:*
Il mio sguardo l'incontr . . .

Alone. One love. One hope. One comfort me. Martha, chest note, return.

—*Come!*

It soared, a bird, it held its flight, a swift pure cry, soar silver orb it leaped serene, speeding, sustained, to come, don't spin it out too long long breath he breathes long life, soaring high, high resplendent, aflame, crowned, high in the effulgence symbolistic, high, of the ethereal bosom, high, of the high vast irradiation everywhere all soaring all around about the all, the endlessnessnessness . . .

—*To me!*

Siopold!

Consumed.

Leon Belly, *The Sirens.* Musee de l'Hotel Sandelin, Saint-Omer, France.

Come. Well sung. All clapped. She ought to. Come. To me, to him, to her, you too, me, us.

In 1917 Franz Kafka (1883–1924) published a short story entitled "The Silence of the Sirens." The author here strikes an unusual chord. His anguish over the absurd and unknown rules and the inclement "silence of God" dispelled, Kafka works with a lightness that is, however, not lacking in a certain irony, mistaking perhaps deliberately in narrating that Ulysses stopped his own ears.

Proof that inadequate, even childish measures may serve to rescue one from peril:

To protect himself from the Sirens Ulysses stopped his ears with wax and had himself bound to the mast of his ship.... The song of the Sirens could pierce through everything, and the longing of those they seduced would have broken far stronger bonds than chains and masts....

Now the Sirens have a still more fatal weapon than their song, namely their silence. And though admittedly such a thing has never happened, still it is conceivable that someone might possibly have escaped from their singing; but from their silence certainly never. Against the feeling of having triumphed over them by one's own strength, and the consequent exaltation that bears down everything before it, no earthly powers could have remained intact.

And when Ulysses approached them the potent songstresses actually did not sing, whether because they thought that this enemy could be vanquished only by their silence, or because the look of bliss on the face of Ulysses, who was thinking of nothing but his wax and his chains, made them forget their singing.

But Ulysses, if one may so express it, did not hear their silence.

But they—lovelier than ever—stretched their necks and turned, let their cold hair flutter free in the wind, and forgetting everything clung with their claws to the rocks. They no longer had any desire to allure; all that they wanted was to hold as long as they could the radiance that fell from Ulysses' great eyes.

If the Sirens had possessed consciousness they would have been annihilated at that moment. But they remained as they had been; all that had happened was that Ulysses had escaped them.

A codicil to the foregoing has also been handed down. Ulysses, it is said, was so full of guile, was such a fox, that not even the goddess of fate could pierce his armor. Perhaps he had really noticed, although here the human understanding is beyond its depths, that the Sirens were silent, and opposed the aforementioned pretense to them and to the gods merely as a sort of shield.

An illustrated Neapolitan fortnightly review published a short story by Maurice Noury in 1932 on the myth of Ulysses and the Sirens. On Ithaca, the survivors of the celebrated adventure pass their old age serenely, comforted every now and then by the sight of their old captain who attempts to rekindle the memories they share. Forias alone, far from being pleased by these encounters, receives Ulysses in the moodiest silence, boiling with rancor.

—Why do you avoid me, Forias? Oh, my old friend! You who were at my side as we came out of the wooden horse, in Ilion! You who slew with one fell stroke the implacable Arthenus? You, my most valorous rower on those voyages over island studded seas. . . .

—Silence!

—For what do you blame me, Forias? Have I not always been just and good?

—During all these endless, unbearable years of uselessness, Ulysses, I have cursed you. Because you have robbed me! You robbed us all, all your seamen!

—Robbed you . . . of what, Forias?

—Of the magic moment . . . of supernatural happiness!

—What do you mean?

—Can't you imagine, *you who heard them?*

—But . . . I don't understand . . .

—The Sirens! . . . Now, do you understand?

Marc Chagall, *The Odyssey*, 1974. The Mourlot-Sorlier Institute, Paris.
© 1997 Artists Rights Society (ARS), NY/ADAGP, Paris.

Before the anger of Forias, the astute Ulysses calmed down, became once more the captain.

—I acted as was fitting. For, had you all listened to them, those bitches, you would have followed their magical call. They would have dragged you and the ship to the bottom of the sea! . .

—What was the difference?

—It would have meant madness and death, I tell you!

—What was the difference?

—Why didn't you go back then, on your own?

—And do you think that I did not? But I never found them. . . .

They were silent. Presently, Ulysses sat on the bench where Forias had been sitting. Like him, he gazed off into the distance, toward the sea. The moon was high in the heavens, and shone in silver petals on the sea. . . . The wind blew through the olive trees making melodious sounds, and everywhere sighs arose. The sound of a shepherd's flute could be heard from the other side of the hill.

—That song, that song, repeated Forias in a low, longing voice, it was so splendid, doesn't just the thought of it arouse in you a voluptuous fear?

—Forgive me, Forias, murmured Ulysses, overcome, defeated.

The poetry of the Argentine Alfonsina Storm (1892–1938), which alternates between infantile singsong and desperate gravity, speaks of the attraction for the sea. Like Virginia Woolf, Storm later committed suicide by drowning.

> *At the bottom of the sea there is a house of crystal.*
> *Toward an avenue of mother-of-pearl it looks.*
> *At five o'clock a large golden fish comes to greet me.*
> *Bringing me a large bouquet of coral flowers.*
> *I sleep in a bed slightly bluer than the sea.*
> *An octopus winks at me through the glass.*
> *In the green wood around me ding dong . . . ding dong.*
> *Sea-green, mother-of-pearl Sirens sing and rock.*
> *And on my head the roughened points of the sea burn.*

Bruno Paul, *The Game of the Blonde and the Brunette*, 1897.

The Uruguayan poet Idea Vilariño (1920–) suffers the eternal conflict between the desire to surrender to the great final mystery and the instinct for self-preservation, which eventually leads her to refuse.

> *Say no*
> *say no*
> *bind me to the mast*
> *but*
> *wishing the wind would hurl it down*
> *and the siren leap aboard and with her teeth*
> *cut the cords and drag me to the depths*
> *saying no no no*
> *but following her.*

Sirens in Literary Theory

Corrado Rosso wrote a book of literary criticism in 1972 entitled *Il Serpente e la Sirena,* in which he shows that both these figures convey an idea of movement. One flees from the serpent toward the Siren, rejecting evil and pain and rushing toward pleasure. It is not, however, so linear as that. In a moment of fear and caution, man halts, possibly even radically changing direction. In the end, a complex mechanism of ambivalence causes a merging of "adversaries," until the Siren incarnates an unnatural paradox: the fear of happiness. "Attraction and repulsion toward happiness; inhibiting fear and idealistic impulse toward the *monstrum fascinans,* toward the Siren." This condition, "olbophobia"—a neologism coined by Rosso—can be said to pervade an important French literary current, including the Enlightenment, Camus, Corneille, Stendhal, Gide, and Alain-Fournier.

Max Horkheimer (1895–1973) and Theodor W. Adorno (1903–1969) wrote jointly during the war, publishing in 1947 their *Dialectic of Enlightenment,* which contains an allegory of Ulysses and the Sirens that is considered a classic in contemporary thought. The direct experience

Advertisement for Perrier mineral water in Télérama, May 22, 1982, Paris.

of Europe, prey to Nazism, and the United States, prey to the industry of culture, led the German thinkers to reflect on the Enlightenment, the scope of which was to liberate humanity from fear and backwardness. In any case, dialectically, it would also imply subjugation, regression. The freedom of Ulysses is dependent on the lack of freedom of the sailors. The Sirens, a force of dissolution, indicate art as knowledge.

Who would survive must not lend their ears to the irrevocable, and this is possible only to the extent that one is incapable of listening. It is that which society has always demanded. Fresh and concentrated, the workers must look ahead, ignoring all that which is peripheral. Impulses which might induce them to deviate must be sublimated—with angry bitterness—in a final effort. They become practical. The other alternative is that chosen by Ulysses, the landed lord, for whom others toil. . . .

The companions who hear nothing, knowing only the danger of the song and not its beauty, leave him bound to the mast, to save him and be saved with him. . . .

Ulysses is substituted in work. How could he not fall prey to the temptation of abandoning himself, thus—in his quality of proprietor—he lacks even participation in work, and—ultimately—even its direction. On the other hand, his companions, as they are closer to things, cannot enjoy work, because it is done under constriction, without prospects, their senses violently dulled. The slave remains subjugated in body and in soul; the master regresses. . . .

Deafness, which has been reserved for the docile proletariat since mythical times, does no good to the master, reduced to immobility.

In *Ulysses and the Sirens,* a study on rationality carried out in 1979 by the Norwegian Jon Elster ranging from the history of economics to sociology and psychology, the attitude of Ulysses before the Sirens is considered emblematic of imperfect human rationality. Conscious of his own weaknesses and having chosen the strategy of the straight line, man has bound himself, obliges himself to use a tactic that, in establishing its limits, prevents him from changing direction. The example can be adapted to unimportant, everyday decisions, to the master plan of capitalism, to efforts to stop smoking, or ban tobacco advertisements, by which we would defend ourselves from the Sirens of advertising. More interesting, however, is one of Elster's comments on seduction:

Persuasion is more similar to seduction than to voluntary choice. . . .
There is no essential difference between coercion and seduction.

2
Fish-Formed Sirens

Genealogy, Relationships, Affinities

While we followed the classic Sirens through to their last evolution, another type emerged that would prevail over all others: the fish-formed Siren. Once the birds' feathers disappeared, the lower part of the new hybrid acquired one or two very visible tail fins. The Sirens became mermaids.

In tracing this astonishing zoological mutation, an intriguing possibility emerges. Perhaps a banal error was made by a scribe, attributable to homophony or paronymy. *Wing* and *fin,* in Greek, are both designated by the same word, *pterughion;* in Latin, only a vowel separates *pennis* and *pinnis.*

Leafing through the works of Baltrusaïtis, that great explorer of forms, one sees that the most inconceivable combinations of animal parts—the most fantastic hybrids—have often been created by imperfect interpretations of ancient texts—quotations from Aristotle or Pliny, the *Physiologous* or Isidor of Seville—being taken literally.

It is precisely in this nomenclature and in these descriptions that the designator finds the reasons for his most absurd compositions in which, literally interpreted, normal specimens became monster. . . . The dolphins which, according to the ancients, were fish with eyes on their backs, mouths on their bellies, and voices similar to human

93

lamentations, are incarnated by the sea sirens, conforming to the definition: faces possessing only the nose, eyes situated behind their shoulders, and jaws with two fangs opening on their chests.

The exceptional nature of this case should not escape us. No centaur, no Sphinx, no dragon ever changed so. This dual representation of the Sirens is one more confirmation of the traditionally dual nature of their symbolism. Their changing form, ready to embrace the newest semblances, is suggestive of uncommon qualities of metamorphosis, which have evolved over the centuries.

From the exterior point of view, the new hybrid has distant ancestors, which could be traced back to Vishnu, seen for the first time by men in the form of a fish after the millennial struggle with Hayagriva, the demon who stole the sacred texts, taking them with him to the bottom of the sea. Or else, even further back in time, to Ea, the lord of the ocean and the abysses, residing in the very dwelling place of knowledge, upon which the earth floats. Ea (*Enki* in Sumerian, *Ea* in Accadian) had a triple nature: human, fish, and goat. A god ruling magic, he taught men the first notions of civilization by means of an incarnation living in

Antonio Rubino, cover of the issue of the magazine *The Graphic Restoration* dedicated to "The Poetry of the Sea," 1907. From the collection of Paola Pallottino.

the Persian Gulf named Oannes. The two entities mingle in that famous figure, half human, half piscine, surrounded by fish, crab, and winged centaur, right hand raised in a gesture of blessing to the Chaldean fleet, in a seventh-century B.C. sculpture in the palace of Sargon II at Korsabad. Often these images are in juxtaposition with those of the Assyrian protector demons, as well as the Apkallu, exorcist priests dedicated to Ea who wore mantles in the form of fish. In the sculptures of Nineveh, Oannes was assimilated into Dagon (*dag,* "fish"), wearing the head of a fish as if it were a miter. It was to this god that the Philistines offered sacrifices as Samson brought down the temple. Oannes eventually evoked two other biblical personages: Jonah, represented almost invariably coming out of the mouth of the whale, forming a single body with the cetacean, and possibly even John the Baptist, who, using liquid consecration, offered admission to a better world. Oannes, Jonah, John: the very homophony of the names help to confirm this derivation.

There is a considerable divergence concerning the female ancestry of the fish-Sirens. Usually, the trail leads back to certain divinities well known at the time of Alexander and venerated subsequently in the temple of Bel at Palmira during the reign of Tiberius. From there, a long sequence of somewhat loose—if not arbitrary—associations begins.

First there was Atargatis the Semitic goddess of the moon, then the

Santuzza Cali and Gabriella Saladino, *Derceto,* 1983; collage in metals, from the exhibit "Metamorphoses." Photograph courtesy of the artists.

Egyptian Hathor of the crescent moon and the Phoenician Astarte, a celestial divinity to whom maidens brought offerings of clothing stained with their menstrual blood. Subsequently came Atar'ata of the Syrians, whom Queen Semiramis herself recommended as an object of devotion, identified by Diodorus Siculus with Derceto. All of these goddesses have been, for one motive or another, seen as one with the Anatolian Magna Mater, the goddess of Byblos, and even Ishtar.

These are preeminently fertility goddesses, the great maternal figures of Asia Minor, almost always carrying a wheat stalk as an attribute, and consequently are closer to Demeter than to the Sirens.

The Syrian goddess Derceto is alone in possessing a fish tail, and then only in the version provided by Diodorus Siculus in his *Bibliotheca*. He tells the following story. By the will of Aphrodite, Derceto was filled with desire for one of her priests, but when the union was consummated and produced its fruit, she was overcome with remorse, killed her lover, and abandoned the female infant in the desert. Then, intent on committing suicide, she threw herself into the waters of Lake Ascalon but only succeeded in obtaining a fish tail as a sign of her transgression. The infant's life was saved by doves, who kept her warm with their feathers and nourished her with milk and cheese brought in their beaks from Simmas, a shepherd of the royal flocks. Later, when informed of her identity, the man adopted her, giving her the name Semiramis. Consequently, both fish and doves were considered sacred by the Syrians.

Lucian (125–192?) described having witnessed the ceremonies of Hierapolis to honor the Dea Syria. Merged with Derceto and Atargatis, she was passed down to the Romans as Diasuria, to be honored together with the Persian Mithras by the cult dedicated to her. Twice a year, pilgrims came to the Syrian city to immerse statues of the goddess, which—as Lucian specifies—represented a woman with no animal features. Her followers were forbidden to eat—or even touch—fish. Lucian explains that Atargatis, pursued by a Lydian called Mopsos, flung herself into the lake, with her son, Ichtye, in her arms. The child drowned, but she, being immortal, lived to see a sanctuary raised in Ascalon in her honor.

Album cover by Peter Barry.

As with Britomartis and Leucothea, we find the continuing motif of deities attempting to save themselves by diving into the water.

In the Hierapolis of Phrygia, Echidna was celebrated as the personification of earthquakes. Since she was represented as a woman with the tail of a serpent, her bodily form was sometimes confused with that of the Sirens, who, however, lost all chthonic aspects.

Continuing with this sequence of analogies, we come to the feminine sea demon defeated by St. Sisinnius of Antinoe, who was martyred during the Diocletian persecutions. Greek legend has it that, while the saint was praying by the Black Sea, a disease-bearing female devil, calling herself the daughter of Herod, appeared to him. He succeeded in convincing her to spare all those who mentioned his name in their prayers. Many early Byzantine lead amulets represent him as similar to Marduk or St. Olaf as he slays the sea woman. The creature defeated by Sisinnius was known to suffocate newborn infants; more recently called Khebat, she would appear to be Halabatu of Aleppo, female equivalent of Hadad, god of the tempests, also known as Alabastu, Labastu (from *abzu,* meaning "depths of the abyss"), Lamia, Labartu, and Lamashtu, the Assyrian enemies of pregnant women and children, who roam at night causing stillbirths.

And here, although made hybrid with a bird and not with a fish, the figure of Lilith once more appears. In the interpretation provided later by the rabbis she was the rebellious first wife of Adam, to whom the angels were sent to drown in the Red Sea. They spared her on the condition that she desist from harming children baptized with their names, because Lilith, inspired by her hatred for the descendants of Eve, had persecuted women in labor and children.

In this vein of feminine associations, through the word *mare* ("sea" in Latin) together with *yam* (the Hebrew word for sea), the Sirens were assimilated with Miriam (pronounced in Arabic "Mar-jam") and, later, the Virgin Mary and Stella Maris ("Star of the Sea").

As with the bird-women, any resemblance to the Sirens is not based on their specific function, only their status as female sea deities. In terms of function there exists instead an evident convergence with the Hindu sea nymphs named Apsaras (from the Sanscript *ap,* "water," and *sara,* "that which moves"). However, these would appear to be much later, as the ancient poet Valmiki does not mention them, reference being made only in an apocryphal book of the *Ramayana.* It tells of the myriad Apsaras generated from the deep foam, splendidly beautiful and decorated with celestial jewels. Musicians and dancers, inhabitants of the waters and the clouds of Indra's heaven, they descend to the earth, in the most unexpected guises, intent on seducing hermits.

Serpentine Siren stabs Adam in the Garden of Eden, from the Vossiani Chymici, Leiden manuscript. Rijksuniversiteit Library, Leiden.

Rock-crystal bottle ornament, sixteenth century. From the shop of Annibale Fontana, Milan.

The Sirens were also associated with Camasenes, the fish-woman to whom Creuzer (1771–1858) briefly refers in his work on religions; with Scylla, who would take on the most sinister and terrifying aspects of the new type; with the Oceanid Psamathe, who transformed herself into a fish to escape the lust of Aeacus but, caught by the Satyr, would conceive Phocus; and with Alabasdria, returned to the Copts with her mother, Antaura, and sometimes represented with the tail of a dolphin or a serpent.

But is it justified to group all these together? Some share the Sirens' relationship with the world beyond, others their aquatic aspect, and few their physiognomy; however, none have been known as having the capacity to seduce with song. Have Aphrodite, Ishtar, Demeter, Mary, and any number of Asiatic or Mediterranean mothers features to identify them with the Sirens?

Transforming the Sirens, who distract men from their duties by offering them other existential choices, to feminine images more complementary to the warrior is one way—and a very successful one—in which they have been made innocuous. As Joyce Lussu suggests, the view of the Sybils as prophetesses and female depositories of wisdom on agriculture, animal breeding, craft, and medicine, who found themselves exiled from power to be thence considered merely mothers or whores, even relegated to a chimeric dimension, is an apt one also for the Sirens.

The Sirens were defeated, as we know, and every defeated divinity either becomes negative or else is so dismembered and encumbered with the attributes and peculiarities of emerging divinities as to be effectively eliminated. Even clinical psychiatrist and Jungian analyst Jean Shinoda Bolen, at the time of writing *Goddesses in Everywoman* (1984), recognized only the victorious classical goddesses of Olympus. Ulysses relates just with Athena and Persephone. Sirius and the dog days—and even the moon—become the exclusive terrain of Artemis, the huntress, armed with bow and quiver. No trace of the Sirens. And yet how many women could have identified with those lost goddesses, bearers of a message to which man is afraid to listen.

Turning now from the Sirens' female lineage, we can recall their male ancestors in the ancient marine pantheon. Their fish form demonstrates their descent from Achelous and their link with Oceanus, Triton, Nereus, Halios, Ponthus, Phorcus, Glaucus, Phalanthus, and Taras the son of Neptune and founder of Tarentum—all half men and half fish. Capricorn might also be included, as his earth association does not prevent his being represented with the tail of a fish, the prize for having found the concha auriculae, which Zeus used in defeating the Titans. In Plato's thought, it is through his constellation that souls enter Hades, while those to be reincarnated leave through the constellation of Cancer. And thus, Capricorn has strong similarities with the Babylonian god Ea, whose task it was to conduct souls to the Fortunatae Insulae. Ea also possessed a goat nature, which, in the Christian Middle Ages, would be attributed to the Devil.

Sirens and Mermaids: Official Birth and Acquired Characteristics

Contrary to what once was commonly believed, fish-formed and winged Sirens shared the same cradle. Two exceptional finds can be considered proof of this: one is a second-century B.C. vase from Megara in the

National Museum of Athens, and the other a first-to-second-century Roman lamp in the Royal Museum of Canterbury. Represented on them are Ulysses and a Siren with a dolphin's tail emerging from the waves, evidence that the later type was also of a Mediterranean origin.

Alexander the Great (356–323 B.C.) was said to have had contact with similar creatures, although strictly speaking they were not Sirens, given that they lacked the seductive gift of song. Examples of the extent to which the exploits of the Macedonian king stimulated the medieval imagination include the writings of the historian Quintus Curtius Rufus (first century A.D.), more romance than chronicle;

Alexander the Great on one of his dives, among fish and amphibian women, fifteenth century, from Manuscript 59 of the *Roman d'Alexandre*. Library of the Petit Palais, Paris. Photograph by Catania.

Alexander's *Letters on the Marvels of India* addressed to his preceptor and friend, Aristotle, but written by the false Callisthenes; and the twelfth-century *Roman* in Alexandrine French verse and the thirteenth-century *Libro* in Alexandrine Spanish verse. Tales abound of the fabulous beings that announced both Alexander's birth and the end of his brief life in Babylon. Alexander himself is said to have succeeded in making the secrets of the air his own and would take off in flight in the company of griffins. In a primitive bathyscaphe, he went in search of the "water of eternal life" and encountered amphibious women perfectly adapted to underwater life. There are paintings from the highlands of Pakistan of women with almond-shaped eyes, long hair, human legs, and a hint of a fin on their elbows, bathing unaware that Alexander is watching them. Others portray bird-Sirens, each on her own branch, listening, entranced, to the words of the conqueror. A sea legend from the Near East tells that some of those Sirens, known as the "sisters of Megalexandros," survived thanks to the "water of eternal life" which they stole. When they learned of the king's death they went mad, overcome with remorse for their theft. One of them took refuge

Edward Munch, *The Lady of the Sea,* 1896.

Leoussis Mastrogannis, *Gorgon,* "Alexander's surviving sister," 1983; Athens postcard.

in the seas of Greece and was called Gorgon, although the term had lost all connection with the snake-haired monsters of antiquity. To all those who passed she asked, in nursery song, whether Alexander was alive. And unfortunate indeed were individuals who failed to give the correct response, for Gorgon would unleash upon them all the fury of her evil powers.

Although full of interpolations, these tales refer to a historical event that had deep and lasting consequences: Alexander's destruction of The-bes. Reacting in anger over the false rumor of his death, he spared only the house of Pindar and the temples.

In the sculpture of the first century B.C., the formal figurative model known as *Chorus Phorci,* where Tritons abounded, was so rampant that Cicero more than once accused the sculptors of Roman fountains of lacking imagination. Horace (65–8 B.C.), in the opening of his *Art of*

Poetry, teases them with a description of an improbable fish-woman, which was extensively quoted, the humor often lacking.

> If a painter chose to join a human head to the neck of a horse, and to spread feathers of many a hue over limbs picked up now here now there, so that what at the top is a lovely woman ends below in black and ugly fish, could you, my friends, if favoured with a private view, refrain from laughing? Believe me, dear Pisos, quite like such pictures would be a book whose idle fancies were shaped like a sick man's dreams, so that neither head nor foot could be assigned to a single shape. "Painters and poets," you say, "have always had an equal right in hazarding anything." We know it: this license we poets claim and in our turn we grant the like; but not so far that savage should mate with tame, or serpents couple with birds, lambs with tigers.

In the same way, his contemporary, Vitruvius, complained about certain figurative styles:

> [Those who] paint on walls nothing but monsters, instead of true and pleasing images. . . . Half figures, some with human faces, others with the heads of animals; all nonexistent things, which could not exist, and which have never existed. . . . Now, despite the obvious falseness of these compositions, instead of being rejected, they are praised, regardless of whether they are possible or impossible things.

Artists are not to blame, however, for the theme is superbly suited to ornament: vibrant, sinuous bodies, contortions, volutes, spiral tails attached to lower human and equine limbs, added to which are the curved forms of the horn, the instrument with which the Tritons calmed the seas or raised tempests.

Equally plastic, it would not be long before the fish-Sirens would be considered the female parallel of the Tritons, and not only physically. Like those great lovers, the Tritons in the sea and the Satyrs on dry land, the Sirens were by then impregnated with eroticism. They were also compared to the Nereids, studied by Propertius (47?–15? B.C.), who calculated that they numbered approximately one hundred—double the number estimated by Hesiod—giving as their distinguishing traits their green hair and fish tails.

But the official birth date of the fish-Sirens, as regards both appearance and function, is established in the *Liber Monstrorum,* an Anglo-Saxon manuscript produced in the eighth or ninth century A.D.

> The Sirens are young sea maidens who seduce sailors with their splendid form and honeyed songs. From head to mid-torso they have female bodies and are in every sense identical to women: however, they have the scaled tails of fish, which they keep well hidden always under water, in the waves.

This casual explanation is, however, impugned a few pages later, under the heading "Scylla." At this point, the *Liber* notes that the girl transformed by Circe into a sea monster for love of Glauce "would be found somewhere between Italy and Sicily, according to the accounts of Gentiles," and that "there, she devoured sailors." After having repeated the description of Virgil, the *Liber* returns to the theme of the Sirens with evident embarrassment because a distinction had to be made.

> Scylla had the head and breasts of a girl, like the Sirens, the abdomen of a wolf and the tail of a dolphin. Another quality distinguishes the Sirens from Scylla: the former ensnare sailors with their fatally dangerous music, while the latter has been seen, surrounded by seals and sea dogs, tearing to bits with violent physical force the wrecked ships and the corpses of the unfortunate mariners.

In English, of course, we have terms to differentiate the two types: *Siren* for the winged women of the Homeric poem and *mermaid* (maid of the sea) when referring to the fish-Sirens. The latter enjoyed such popularity in Britain as to be commonly referred to as "Celtic Sirens." In fact, one of the earliest mentions of mermaids—the legend of the Lake of Belfast—is in the story of an Irish saint. The young Liban, whose entire family had perished during the flood of 90 B.C., somehow succeeded in remaining afloat for a very long time. Fortunately, she eventually sprouted a salmon's tail, and her faithful companion was transformed into a sea lion. Thus, they were both able to adapt perfectly to the sea environment and enjoyed exceptional longevity. After many centuries—in the year A.D. 558—fishermen, attracted by her magic song, captured the Siren in their net, baptized her with the name of Murgen (born of the sea), and began carting her about in a tank of water to be displayed as a carnival freak. Many miracles were attributed to her, and it was believed that the Irish saint Congal, of the Order of Bangor, interceded with the divine powers to have her ascend to heaven.

Anglo-Saxon tradition, despite the Roman lamp in the Museum of Canterbury that proves the Mediterranean origin of the fish-Siren, considers her to be a native of the Isle of Man. The Company of Fishermen, founded in the sixth century A.D., chose the mermaid as their emblem, and when one of their members dies he lies in state in Fishmongers' Hall in a pall richly embroidered with her figure.

The mermaids' relationship with man is probably so positive because their destiny is intertwined with that of the fairies, an eminently Celtic invention. "Rapid as thought," was Hamlet's admiring comment. Phrases such as "Meremaides be here," which until recently were found on maps, were less meant as warnings against danger than to counsel prudence with guns: besides being very skillful in dodging bullets, Sirens can retaliate when provoked by shaking the boat. A law on the books in England until the twentieth century claimed for the crown "all mermaids found in British waters."

In the Shetland Islands, mermaids are stunningly beautiful women who live under the sea; their hybrid appearance is temporary, the effect being achieved by donning the skin of a fish. They must be very careful not to lose this while wandering about on land, because without it they would be unable to return to their underwater realm. Another branch, the Irish *moruadh,* uses a hat as a safe-conduct.

It is worth noting the affection with which William Butler Yeats treats the mermaids in his collection of fairy tales from the Irish oral tradition. He fuses Celtic paganism with the devils and saints of Christian tradition and colors them with romanticism. Here is how he delineates the water fairy archetype:

> Sometimes they come out of the sea, and wander about the shore in the shape of little hornless cows. They have, when in their own shape, a red cap, called a *cohullen druith*, usually covered with feathers. If this is stolen, they cannot again go down under the waves.
>
> Red is the colour of magic in every country, and has been so from the very earliest times. The caps of fairies and magicians are well-nigh always red.

The Sirens of the lakes of Scotland have their own name: they are called kelpies. One of them even became infatuated with a monk, and for that reason was continuously running aground. The holy man, however, resisted her advances with the excuse that he first had to learn how to live under water. As this was impossible, the mermaid resigned herself

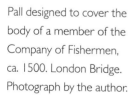

Pall designed to cover the body of a member of the Company of Fishermen, ca. 1500. London Bridge. Photograph by the author.

to giving him up, although she was consumed with grief. Her tears were transformed into those gray-green pebbles that the Scots call "mermaids' tears." A natural abode for Sirens also exists in Scotland, at the famous basalt grotto of Fingal on the island of Stafia, where the sea produces masterful musical sounds.

Geographically, the Sirens spread even to the northernmost regions, demonstrating that they can adapt even to seas where they cannot count on the complicity of the dog-day heat. The Margygr, the famed Scandinavian mermaid, preserves the memory of Latin seas only in her name, for her body consists of an equine head, protruding ears like horns, two stumps for arms, swelling breast, short hands with webbed fingers, cetacean or serpent's tail. With such oddities, it is difficult to see what esthetic value her green eyes, flowing hair, or powerfully attractive voice could have. King Olaf of Norway (995?–1030), in his piratical escapades, encountered and killed a Margygr, running it through with a long spear. Many are inclined to interpret this event as an allegory in which the defeated Siren represents paganism, which the Viking king, a future saint, was obliged to annihilate.

Sirens in the Bestiaries and Art of the Middle Ages and the Renaissance

Departing from the *Liber*, medieval bestiaries continued to make entries under the heading "Siren," often less than rigorously, at times moved by the fever for cataloging. Frequently, tales were padded out with the

Richard de Fournival, illustration from the *Bestiaire de l'Amour*, 1250. Bibliotheque Nationale, Paris.

Sacramentary of Gellone,
Visigothic manuscript in Latin,
end of the eighth century.
Bibliotheque Nationale, Paris.
Photograph from the collection
of Aldo Zita.

deeds of Alexander the Great and St. Olaf or travel accounts of such as St. Brendan, the Irish monk who situated Paradise in the Atlantic and recorded his wanderings around the world in drawings.

Sirens are the principal iconographic subject in illuminated manuscripts: between the lines, in the ornamenting of initial letters and headings, in the margins of maps, in wood engravings. They abound in heraldic crests and coats of arms. In tribute to their regal dignity so difficult to erase, they are represented wearing crowns. Paradoxically,

The ideal of heraldry, from the
Encyclopedia Espasa Calpe, Madrid.

Pantaleone, detail of a floor mosaic in the Cathedral of Otranto, 1167. Photograph by Raffaele Perelli.

their empire is now in the medieval cathedrals, where they have been immortalized in sculptures on portals, capitals, choir pews, and holy water stoups, or in the colors of mosaics and stained glass. Romanesque Sirens look outward, absorbed and implacable as idols, as if singing a last warning to the faithful who enter the sacred space.

In mystical zoology, various animals, both those of proven biological existence and the purely imaginary type, symbolize vice and virtue. In order to stigmatize the Sirens and associate them with the world of sin and damnation, bestial elements are made to emerge in every possible variation and combination: barbarous and thickset those of

Siren with tails terminating in pinecones. Saint Michael's Cathedral, Pavia. Photograph by Aldo Sita.

Saint-Germain-des-Près in Paris; soft and pleasing those of the cathedral of Modena, among the earliest representations. Exemplary is the Siren depicted in the floor mosaics of the Cathedral of Otranto, in true Romanesque style: in a tondo, with small, threadlike plaits and heavy earrings, surrounded by Solomon and a mounted bugler, an octopus, and an ostrich.

We see them accompanied by lions and unicorns, Harpy, Sphinx, Hydra, Gorgon, Phoenix, two-faced Janus, Argo of the hundred eyes, bucranes and rams, acrobats, asses playing harps, centaurs, chimeras, basilisks, salamanders, dragons, and unknown varieties of mythical fauna. Some are asymmetrical with a single tail; others possess axial symmetry with a double tail. They are inscribed in circles, semicircles, squares, quatrefoils, lozenges, omegas, and crosses. They are alone or in pairs, facing or back-to-back, triple or in entangled masses that form, consolidate, dissolve into a succession of vegetal or animal mutations. Their tails are at times terminated by pinecones, which indicate permanence because the resin prevents the decomposition of tissue, or else irises, flower-sprigs, vine tendrils, or feral heads. Tails can be massive legs or stylized, lilied, double-crenellated, double-forked fish bones. For the first time, Sirens with the tail of a serpent, an iniquitous sign of their diabolical aspect, are seen. Human feet accompany the flapping fish

Siren nursing infant, capital in the Cathedral of Our Lady of Love, Freiburg, thirteenth century. Photograph by Tristan Cotté.

Sirens playing a vielle and holding an infant; bas-relief, 1310. Cathedral of St. Jean, Lyons. Photograph by Gustin.

tail. Smooth bodies and ashlar-worked scales and other combinations, fusions, eccentricities, phantasmagorias, and obsessions appear.

A new characteristic pose is at this point adopted by the bicaudal Sirens: gathering up their two extremes symmetrically in a highly feminine gesture, as though lifting the hems of their skirts not to drag them. It is interesting here to consider a comment made by Cirlot, who suggests that the turned-up tail is an infernal parody of arms raised in adoration. At times, close to the Sirens thus represented, human women are portrayed holding up their ankles, their legs raised outward in the same way. Even their hairstyle, reminiscent of barbarians, imitates the same movement with two bands pulled to the sides.

In some examples, artists portray the Sirens in the role of nurse, holding their infants. We might cite the sculptures in the cathedrals of Cologne, Auxerres, and Beauvais (the Siren with the folds on her abdomen would appear to have repeatedly given birth), Freiburg (where the infant holds a bird), Basel (here it holds a fish), and Lyons (here, in bas-relief, stands a family trio: a crowned Siren to the right holding her infant, and to the left, playing the vielle, a symmetrical figure made ambiguous by erosion, either another Siren or a bearded Triton who would obviously be the father of the creature).

Often the later model alternates with the ancient one: bird-women in the text, fish-women in the illustrations, as in facsimiles of the famous *Physiologous,* which originally contained only the winged women. This we see in both the ninth-century Bern manuscript, which was the work of the School of Rheims, and the fourteenth-century Brussels manuscript. Depicted in the latter are sailors in a catatonic sleep and a female creature named "Serre" who has many wings at her wrists and a tail lilied at the end. The two traditions also exist side by side in the *Bestiaire Divin* (1211) of Guillaume le Clerc of Normandy:

> *The siren, who sings so sweetly*
> *And enchants folk by her song*
> *Affords example for instructing those*
> *Who through this world must voyage.*
> *We who through the world do pass*
> *Are deceived by such a sound,*
> *By the glamour, by the lusts*
> *Of this world, which kill us*
> *When we have tasted such pleasures.*
> *Wantonness and bodily ease,*
> *And gluttony and drunkenness,*
> *Slothfulness and riches,*
> *Palfreys, fat horses,*
> *The splendor of rich draperies*
> *So great is our delight in them*
> *That perforce we fall asleep.*
> *Thereupon the siren kills us.*

In the *Otia Imperialis,* which appeared between the twelfth and thirteenth centuries, Gervais follows the theme of the *Physiologous;* however, he changes the word *bird* to *fish.* With the figurative sense lost, a truly blood-curdling image results.

> At that point were they attacked by sirens, who threw themselves upon their bodies, tearing their flesh and devouring them.

It was left to the *Bestiaire de l'Arsenal* (ca. 1214), which still follows the *Physiologous,* to confirm this psychological trait in the Sirens and also to determine the current types: two formed like fish—with single or double tail—and one winged, with which the illustrations accurately correspond. A few decades later, Richard de Fournival would offer the same version in his *Bestiaire d'Amour.*

> There are three forms of siren, two of which are half woman and half fish, and the other half woman and half bird. All three types sing, one with a horn, one with a harp, the last with voice alone. And their melodies are so pleasing that no one, upon hearing them, can resist following them. And when man is captured, he falls into slumber. And when they find him asleep, they kill him.

An illustration in the *Cambridge Bestiary,* unlike the description, presents a figure of a woman from the waist up with the enormous claws of a bird of prey, a fish tail, and a short skirtlike garment halfway between scale and feather. She holds a fish in her right hand and her own tail fin in her left.

In his *Tesoretto,* Brunetto Latini (1220?–1294) considers the Sirens diverse, both in their physical aspect and their music, and proposes

"Serre," *Brussells Manuscript,* fourteenth century.

once more that they be called harlots. In this, at least, he differs from his pupil, Dante, who was to confer considerably different epithets on the Sirens.

> The Sirens, say the authors, are in three manners, having the appearance of women from their heads to their thighs, but from that point down have the appearance of fish, wings and claws. The first sang marvellously with the mouth and voice of a woman, the second with the voice of a flute and in polyphony, the last with a small horn, and with their sweet song they caused the ingenuous mariner to perish. But, in truth, the Sirens were three strumpets who drained man, reducing him to poverty. And history tells us that they had wings and claws, symbolizing love which flies and wounds; and they lived in the water since lasciviousness was made up of moisture.

Guido de Columnis (1210–1280) of Messina rewrote in Latin prose the *Roman de Troie* by Benoît de Sainte-Maure. The fish-Sirens, by that time

Arnold Böcklin, *Calm at Sea*, 1886.

thoroughly established, once again entered the narration of the return of Ulysses to Ithaca, but this more modern version bore important changes.

> The song so inebriates the souls of the unfortunate seamen that they, upon hearing it, throw off the weight of all preoccupation, as its sweetness caresses their hearing, causing them practically to forget themselves, no longer eating or drinking, while a torpor alights upon their souls and they fall into a deep sleep. When the Sirens see them sleeping, they overturn the ships which, without their helmsmen, sink. Thus, the seamen drown in their sleep. I encountered these Sirens and, to avoid my companions being ensnared, I stopped up my ears and theirs, so as not to hear anything of their song, and this way my companions and I defeated them.
>
> We killed more than a thousand of them, after which we passed their island unscathed, the danger past.

Cambridge Bestiary, twelfth century.
Courtesy of Franco Maria Ricci.

The seventeenth-century author of *Emblems,* Jean Baudoin, presents a winged Orpheus, erect and holding a lyre, with a bicaudal Siren on the ground. For him, the Sirens represent voluptuousness, the proof of which is their choosing as their dwelling place a secluded, delightful island, obviously with the intention of abandoning themselves to pleasure in absolute freedom. Baudoin informs us also that the Sirens did not always sing the same melody but directed to each passerby the music they judged most likely to induce their surrender. Because the Sirens were overcome by the praises shouted to the immortal gods by Orpheus, Baudoin's discourse concludes:

> We draw the moral that meditations on the divine surpass in sweetness and in power all the pleasures of our senses.

During the Renaissance, the Sirens lurked everywhere. They arrogantly entered heraldry, from the crests of the port cities to noble escutcheons, and learned to meander down unusual streets, carved on the handles of canes and sleighs. Above all, they became a favorite motif for the figureheads of ships. Attached to the prow, they too sail, fending off the winds and waters. Blue and gold, like madonnas, they are a favorite subject for the artisans of every marine people.

At this time when mastery of the seas was increasing, the cosmographers still decorated their renderings of the earth's surface with sinuous figures of Sirens. The phrase *hic sunt leones*—"here be lions"—was placed in the very center of maps of Africa to convey the impression of the mystery and dangers of unexplored lands. *Hic sunt sirenae* was used in the same way to mark unexplored waters.

In illustrated texts from the fields of human learning, from natural history to philosophy, from theology to occult studies, the fish-Sirens became so profuse as to obscure the classical winged model. They are to be found in the limelight, starting from the extravagant aquatic spectacles of the Baroque period, in the Florence of the Medici and the Parma of the Farnese, in the French *Ballet de Cour* and the English masque. *Circe,* the seminal *Ballet Comique de la Reine,* was created in Paris in

Bridge of the Little Mermaids, constructed in 1842 from the plans of architect Francesco Tettamanzi over the San Damiano Canal in Milan. The mermaids were jokingly called "le ghisine" (the little cast-iron girls) because it was the first time that cast iron had been used in Milan. Photograph by Stelio Vinanti.

1581 by Balthazard de Beaujoyeux. It was presented in the large Salle Bourbon of the Louvre with the scenography of Jacques Patin, which called for ten wagons, some of which were actually mobile fountains. The most dazzling was the one carrying Neptune, played by King Charles IX himself. After the scene with Circe and a prisoner, the Sirens and the Tritons appeared, singing. Judging from the sketches, the former wore costumes with voluminous tails and carried hand mirrors; the latter, similarly costumed, held musical instruments and tridents. After six hours of performance, the *deus ex machina* arrived, with Jove freeing everyone while the ladies, illustrious gentlemen, and sovereigns on stage exchanged reverences.

New Attributes, New Symbols, New Associations

All ornithological traces lost, the sea element became accentuated in the fish-Sirens. Away from the air, which gives lightness and like fire tends upward, their point of reference became mainly water, the element that like the earth tends downward. The concept of flight eliminated, what prevailed was the fall: the painful experience of the child, the nightmare of man. The *Liber Exceptionum* of St. Victor used this air/water polarity as an ethical homily:

Esther Williams in the 1952 movie *Million Dollar Mermaid.* Courtesy of Ugo Casiraghi.

Birds flying signified the contemplation of the celestial by which man rises above the inferior. . . . Fish signified the villains, since they never left the place where they were created. . . . The upper waters signified the good who merit salvation, and the lower waters the bad who deserve damnation. But what are these waters? The unclean, the fornicators, concubines, the incestuous, adulterers, misers, thieves, predators, drunks, perjurers, the hateful, murderers, and those for whom woman is an object of concupiscence.

Water is the dominion of fish, which, unlike other animals, we picture in all roles, as they devour or are devoured, as dictated by the strong interdependence that exists in the aquatic realm. And the fish—the term here intended in the broad sense, with sea fauna and sea mammals included—is another ancient symbol loaded with values and, as we have seen, sacred and untouchable for the Syrian goddess Derceto.

Elevated to Christian emblem, we find the fish among the earliest

Fish, anchor, and cross in the graffiti of the catecombs of Saint Priscilla; archives of the Benedictine Sisters in Rome.

miracles of the Nazarene, in the apostles who were fishermen, in the water and wine of early Christian mystery, drawn in the graffiti of the catacombs where it also appears in writing through the word *ichthys,* forming the acrostic in Greek for Jesus Christ Son of God the Savior. Tertullian (155? B.C. to after A.D. 220), regarded as the most important Western apologist, in a famous allegory refers to Christians as small fish born of the great fish, Jesus Christ; only by remaining in water—that is, in the state of grace that baptism confers—will they find salvation.

Certain authors argue that the Sirens, with both human and fish aspects, represent the passage from days on which it was permitted to eat meat to fast days. But they are generally considered to be at the opposite

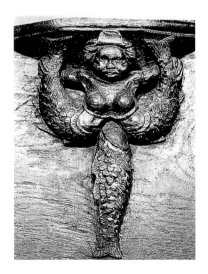

Siren with fish in her vagina, sculpted on one of the benches of the Church of Saint Thiebault, Thann, fifteenth century. Photograph by Gustin.

Siren using fish as clubs against the fishermen, great door of the Cathedral of Cunault.

pole from Christ the Fisherman. They too catch the faithful fish who approach and demand proof from them, but instead of elevating the fish to the heavens and offering them eternal life, they plunge them into the dark abyss of the sea. We see Sirens brandishing fish like clubs and threatening sailors in the cathedral at Cunault. We see them strangling fish, squeezing their gills at St. Germain-des-Prés, hitting them with a

Sirens ready to tempt the survivors of the Flood, Nuremburg Bible, 1493.

Serpentine Siren tormenting a flagellant Christ; Manuscript 428 of Saint Gallen, Kantonsbibliothek, Vadiana.

cudgel (Echillais, Santonge), disembowelling them with knives (Montagne, Poitou), and one holding them in her vagina at Thann, either because she is giving birth to the fish or else using them as blasphemous instruments of masturbation. We see them swimming in the waters of the Great Flood, awaiting the survivors of the Ark. In some images the fish-women merge with the serpent-women: we see them as accomplices of Eve, piercing Adam with the dagger of eternal death (see page 98) or tormenting the flagellant Christ.

In alchemy, on the contrary, the Sirens were considered a positive symbol. As the union of fish (rising sulfur) and the virgin (common mercury), they embodied the philosophical mercury or salt of

Alchemical Siren from *Azoth des Philosophes,* by Basil Valentine, 1659, Paris.

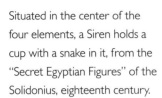

Situated in the center of the four elements, a Siren holds a cup with a snake in it, from the "Secret Egyptian Figures" of the Solidonius, eighteenth century.

knowledge. Above all, the Sirens connoted the supreme conjunction of opposites, the alchemical intention of rendering external that which is internal, spiritual that which is corporeal, metaphysical that which is natural. In this sense they can be associated with Trismegistus and the works of Albert the Great, scholar of the process of purification of mercurial waters; in the *Hortus Sanitatis* (1485), somewhere between a bestiary and a pharmaceutical handbook; in the seventeenth-century *Mutus Liber,* which contains a small Siren moving on the black wave of the third and final circle; and in Basil Valentine's *Azoth des Philosophes* (1659), featuring a Siren from whose breasts the sun and the moon pour forth in streams of gold and silver.

Among the many alchemical representations of Sirens, the most famous is the figure known as the *Anima Mercurii,* taken from the *Solidonius,* an eighteenth-century manuscript. This Siren wears a heavy crown and has long, flowing hair covering her back; her wings are spread, her tail ends in a double fluke, and in her right hand is a goblet containing a serpent and surrounded by the four elements, among which the earth appears as a flowering island. Jung considered this figure to be the *Anima Mundi,* condensing the dual feminine motif of Eden; for Klossowski it was the synthesis between the destructive woman and her counterpart, knowledge. In oneiric and alchemist symbolism, the transformation from human into fish became a metaphor for entering the unconscious world of dreams, inebriation, and death. It is also symbolic of regression to a primitive state, the Heraclitan hypothesis that men descended from fish having been reasserted by modern biology. And, lastly, there are the considerable psychoanalytical implications attached to the fish; for the Freudian Roheim, for example, the fusiform tail is a powerful phallic symbol, and the Sirens, by exhibiting a tail-penis when the male expects to see a vulva, become the image of the phallic woman.

We can exclude the possibility that, in the course of their evolution, Sirens regressed from warm-blooded birds to cold-blooded fish; instead, from the form of the tail, dolphins—sea mammals—seem to be responsible for this new hybrid, a fact with numerous implications.

An animal venerated by the ancient Greeks, the dolphin was also dear to Apollo to whom, in that form, a sanctuary was dedicated at Delphi. With its darting, compact body, the dolphin asserted itself by its playful character, its passion for music, and its gestures of friendship to those about to be overwhelmed by the sea. The constellation of the dolphin in the heavens, according to the ancients, is the proof of Zeus's recognition of that generosity.

Siren trumpeter, detail from *The Triumph of Neptune,* from a fifteenth-century book of paintings.

Siren harpist,
seventeenth-century woodcut.

If the Sirens were the result of a hybridization with the dolphin, this, in addition to physical strength, would also have passed on to them new psychological qualities, such as cheerfulness and openness to mortal humans. A mysterious link also binds the dolphin to the feminine. In Greek, *delphis* signifies cetacean (large fish); *delphoi,* the place of Apollo's cult; and *delphys,* the uterus or vulva. The latter connection had already been documented by Hippocrates and Aristotle.

The transition from bird-women to sea-maids complete, the Sirens continued to hold musical instruments, but they now included the horns, lutes, and vielles of the times. Their hands sometimes held fish, oars, and fans, but above all, two new objects destined to become their inseparable attributes: the mirror and the comb.

The flat surface of the water is the original mirror. Entering this terrain, one inevitably turns to Carl Jung.

He who looks into the "mirror" of water sees first of all his own image. He who goes towards himself risks meeting himself. The mirror does not flatter: it shows accurately that which is being reflected, that is the face which we never reveal to the world, because we conceal it behind the *persona,* the actor's mask. . . . The encounter with

English woodcut, sixteenth century.

oneself is one of the most unpleasant of experiences, from which we flee, projecting all that which is negative onto the world around us.

Flat, smooth sea; reflective, iridescent surfaces: the Sirens embrace myriad meanings associated with the natural mirror of water but no less so with the artificial mirror they now possess. The mirror deforms or, better still, metamorphoses. The looking glass, the implement the sea-men of the Mediterranean use in the night to find and attract fish; the burning glass, as dazzling as the Platonic diamond spheres where stood the eight Sirens; the speculum, the "mirror" that explores the darkest cavities of the woman's body. That of the Sirens is a hand mirror, a circle on a cross, graphic symbol of the planet Venus, a symbol that also indicates the female sex. Thus, the mirror, although a new attribute, does no more than confirm the Sirens' birthright, which is belonging to the fluid element, their luminous and at the same time dark character, the innermost aspect of the feminine.

In addition, with their mirrors the Sirens look at themselves, study their own appearance; speculate, in the sense of searching, examining, investigating, sounding, scrutinizing, meditating. This literal "self-reflection" has as its goal *knowing,* as was implicit in the classical Sirens, who tantalized others with their knowledge.

We know that Dionysus, the divine child, was murdered by the Titans while he was immersed in his own reflection, a terrible act of knowledge that Giorgio Colli translates in these terms:

Mirroring oneself, manifesting and expressing oneself; knowing is nothing else. . . . Only
Dionysus exists; we and our world are his
false appearance, that which he sees when he
places himself before the mirror.

The mirror is also illusion and lends itself
easily to illusionism. It represents the double,
the shadow: the soul outside the body. Those
who would evoke the spirits use smooth surfaces: mirrors, spheres, crystal cups, swords.
With the game of mirrors, one can even
deceive skylarks. With the aid of a mirror Perseus was able to slay Medusa; with the instrument used to mirror themselves, the Sirens can
also dazzle man.

Ovid envisioned the nymph Salmacis gaz-
ing at her reflection in the natural mirror of
the surface of her pool, languorously combing her hair, until the appearance of the youth
Hermaphroditus, with whom she merges in a
total fusion.

In *Iconologia*, a treatise from the sixteenth
century, Cesare Ripa of Perugia considered
the ways Sirens were represented, interpret-
ing colors, positions, and other noteworthy
things and concluded that in depicting the

Paolo Belluso, the passage from stiletto
heels to fins, from clinging dresses to a
pisciform body, from woman to mermaid,
1984. Courtesy of the artist.

Sirens, the ancients had already included the element of deceit. Subsequently, his contemporaries, in portraying them with mirrors, were simply reinforcing the sense of their mendacity.

> Falsity of love, or deceit. Woman superbly dressed or Siren looking into a mirror. The mirror is the true symbol of falsity, because although it appears to reflect all which is placed before it, it is only a similitude, possessing no reality, in which the left hand becomes the right, and right becomes left.

In other words, the mirror, an object as extraordinary as the Sirens and as ambiguous, offers truth and deception, obvious proof and duplicity. Thus, Jacques Bril could deduce:

> Every mirror is magic because every mirror is a "trap for souls" and it is these instruments of autistic regression which those man-eaters carry with them.

And so the sense of sight is sharpened to the detriment of the sense of hearing, opening the way for the important component of voyeurism. Now the Sirens seduce with their bodily presence alone. Now it is essential that they be seen.

The Sailors' Trap, seventeenth century, from "The World of the Incredible."

The Erynyes and the Gorgons, who were not made for seduction, are distinguished by a head of ruffled, disorderly hair, a sign that they belong to chaos, or at least to a feral, alien, and undesirable world. In contrast, long and flowing, silky and sinuous hair cannot fail to attract. Thus, besides the mirror, the Sirens have also armed themselves with the comb. The waves of their hair are entwined with the waves of the sea, with the waves of matter itself. Ripples of waves, sonorous waves, luminous waves, undulating and regular sinusoid design: pure sound, pure light.

After being depicted with raven Mediterranean hair on Greek, Etruscan, and Roman vases and in Christian imagery for ten centuries, the Sirens became predominantly blond, perhaps with the emergence of the Celtic mermaid. Combing their wet hair, the Sirens produce gleaming iridescences. Their hair itself echoes the liquid element, flowing over their shoulders like a waterfall. The comb evokes water, like the fish bone, itself used as an early comb. This fundamental graphic sign, a horizontal line with vertical ones descending from it, was used by several ancient agricultural civilizations to indicate water falling from the clouds. Combing their hair, the Sirens scatter drops of water. At this point, a comment of Gilbert Durand comes to mind, for the endless motifs it suggests:

The hair is not connected to water because it is feminine, but is made feminine because it is the hieroglyphic for water, water which manifests in menstrual blood.

Mermaid with comb and mirror; bas-relief in wood on the partition between stalls, fifteenth century. Saint Peter's Cathedral, Saint-Claude, Jura.

Erich Neumann also stressed the close relationship that exists between the mysteries of feminine transformation and the water element, whether menstrual blood or amniotic fluid or mother's milk.

In Greek *kteis,* in Latin *pecten,* and in archaic Italian *pettignone,* the word *comb* also designates the pubis. In the same way, the sea mollusk—called *pettine* in Italy and known in Galicia as *venera*—recalls the form of the female genitals. The comb untangles hair and cards wool, conveying the hirsute, which leads back to animality, animal sensuality. Most evocatively, the French word for the flax comb, a tool used to align and refine flax fibers, is *séran*. Roheim argues that the bird-women storming around Ulysses, who was standing stiff as a rod, were representations of the orgasm and that the comb of the fish-women was linked to pubic hair or, more specifically, masturbation.

These fish-Sirens were impregnated with a sexuality totally absent in the primitive ones. Remember how Aphrodite punished them precisely for their stubborn refusal to have sexual relations with anyone, be they gods or mortals? In matters related to the sexual sphere, the ancients looked to Eros or Aphrodite, who could become Urania when the eroticism was more intellectual or Pandemus when related to immediate physical

Sirens playing bagpipes, horn, trumpet marine, and vielle; fresco on the crossed vaults of the ground-floor salon of the Bishop's Palace at Beauvais, ca. 1350.

desire. Lack of restraint was attributed to Silenus or Satyrs, to Maenads or nymphs.

Now the symbol became flesh. It no longer enjoyed the abstract dignity, the allure of knowledge, with which it had been conferred by the ancient philosophers. The animal aspect prevailed, and this inferior, baser part had to be subdued. In addition, the Sirens were pictured using musical instruments forbidden by the church for appealing to the lower instincts, the same instruments once ascribed to Dionysus. But their music counted less as their ways of seduction grew merely sexual.

Yemanjá, the African American sea goddess, who today still boasts a multitude of followers, provides a clear example of this process. This Yoruba Siren does not sing but listens to the words that all her followers know by heart and sing in chorus:

> *Yemanjá, come, come from the sea . . .*
> *Siren, siren, come let's play in the sand . . .*
> *The siren of the sea has appeared,*
> *the siren wants to play . . .*
> *How sweet to die among the waves . . .*

On the second day of February a follower of Yemanjá throws an offering into the sea in Salvador Bahia, 1990. Photograph by Patrizia Giancotti.

A simple shout without music salutes her: *Him-hi-Yemin*. To entrance men, the force of her femininity is all that is needed. Folco Quilici, a skin diver who has bathed in many seas, believes that Yemanjá symbolizes a relationship of beauty and carnal union with the liquid element, which also implies the fear of the abyss. He writes:

> Only the votaries of Yemanjá know the truth of this relationship, and have always known it; they learned it during their days and nights at sea. They are the keepers of that secret: they are those old and young who plunge into the water from boats, even at night when the ocean is horribly deep. We can see, observe, analyze, interpret: but only they can know. They, the old and young sailors and fishermen, subjects and lovers of the monster, are the only ones in the world admitted to the love of the divine siren of death, whose beautiful body consisting of foam, reflections and dragon scales appears immortal, as in all fables of terror, born with us and which will never abandon us.

The Sirens represent nothing less than the female sex: sea grotto, fissures, crevices, fearful ravines covered by seaweed. Added to the fear of

Serpent-Siren with exposed sex, on a stall in the Church of Saint Sulpice, Diest, 1491.

The Gotaplatsen Fountain in Goteborg, designed by Carl Milles in 1931. Photographs by Leo Rossiello Ramirez.

falling is the fear of the womb, which Gilbert Durand calls a "microcosm of the abyss, symbolic of the fall in miniature."

Some will point out that although the Sirens embody female sexuality, they lack a literal vagina. Yet some legends speak of Sirens that possess a small opening for carnal congress, who have been known to marry common mortals, procreate, and nurse their infants. The bicaudal Sirens in particular do not seem to differ from human women in their reproductive organs. Even the iconography at times shows them with their tails opened out, more indicative of sexual exhibitionism than any deficiency.

One finds female genitalia on a Siren at Westminster, and on the Serpent-Siren in the church of St. Sulpice. At St. Thiebault in Thann there is the figure of a Siren with a fish in her vagina (see page 120). A less extreme example is offered in a work by Rubens: the women who attend the landing of Marie de Médicis at Marseilles have feet in the form of fish; in every other respect they resemble the Flemish master's usual nude female figures (see page 134).

In most cases, however, the Siren is a sex symbol that lacks the essential organ. What is the meaning of this contradiction? Is it an example of their ambiguous nature? Or has the Siren become another casualty of man's anxiety toward female sex?

Peter Paul Rubens, *Disembarcation of Marie de Médicis at Marseilles*, seventeenth century. Louvre, Paris. Photograph by Chuzeville.

More than once in the *Fleurs du Mal,* an "abominable book" as Baudelaire himself described it, the Siren, who enters with her all-embracing softness, inspires at the same time terror and desire:

> *Voluptuousness, always be my queen!*
> *Take the mask of a Siren*
> *made of velvet and flesh. . . .*
>
> *My nightmare, ungirt Siren*
> *that pulls me, always upright at my side,*
> *by my saint's habit*
> *to offer me the poison of a shameless love.*

Even for men free of religious preconceptions, the Sirens continue to represent the dark lady and must be imagined as creatures whose

David Delamare,
Bathing in Moonlight,
1993. © 1994
David Delamare,
Portland, Oregon.

upper bodies awaken a desire that their lower parts are incapable of satisfying—the metaphor of the impenetrable feminine made literal. As always, they are objects of attraction and anguish, but now an additional level of mystery is added: wondering whether they possess female genitalia is more troubling than knowing either way. Whatever the case, whether in excess or lacking, virtual or real, a new, disturbing sexuality is now attributed to the Sirens.

With their incriminating part perennially immersed in the water, the Sirens reveal another concept known as the rejection of the wet, similar to the rejection of the tongue—which in early Christian times represented a world of iniquity and contamination. Remember the letters of Paul to the Romans and to the Corinthians and the universal letter of James: orality must be opposed as demonic, the tongue being an organ impossible to control. One of the first to shed light on the moist quality of the female and lustful aspect of the Sirens was Brunetto Latini. Perhaps due to the liquid emissions that usually accompany nervous crises, the Sirens came to inspire the same misogynist reactions as did witches and hysterics—two other groups whose stories we receive through the interpretation of men. They are the dark women, the incomprehensible and threatening that is feared in female nature.

It comes as no surprise that these feared women—once associated with Sirius and the dog days, noon and the serene sunlit sky—came under the aegis of the moon, which controls the waters and female ovulation. No longer a part of the eternal luminous present of Ananke and the eight spheres and the music that expressed it, they exist now in the measured cycles of the moon with its equally set cadences. And what is music if not the illusion of manipulating time? What is music if not time organized into sounds and silences? But even this music is lost now, for the Sirens have stopped singing to us.

Sirens in Religious Rites

At present, the Americas are the center of the cult of the Sirens. The Inuit culture, for so long misnamed Eskimo, venerates Sedna, a woman-

Pudlat Pudlo, *Sedna Carrying a Fish Man*, 1960; small statue in opaque green and gray steatite. Cape Dorset, Canada.

seal hybrid, goddess of the sea. When, around A.D. 1000, the Inuit peoples settled among the glaciers of the Canadian Arctic and as far north as Greenland, the shamans went into a trance courting the greatest of dangers in order to evoke Sedna. They made her promise to render the sea animals docile, so that men could more easily capture them and nourish themselves. According to their legends, Sedna was a maiden, but because of an act of transgression, the blood-drenched memory of which has been lost, her fingers were cut off and thrown into the glaciers, where she now

Taleelayu, *Sedna;* lithograph. Courtesy of Dorset Fine Art, Toronto, Canada.

rules. From her severed digits came all species of acquatic animals as well as the Inuit, who consider themselves children of the sea.

Sedna comes onto the shore when her initiates invoke her in ceremonies of collective possession. She must have total darkness, accustomed as she is to the polar abysses. The shaman attempts to stop her with a harpoon, while the adepts abandon themselves in erotic dances. When the light returns, Sedna disappears, but no one doubts her visit for there are fresh traces of her blood on the shaman's harpoon.

The Siren of the Americas par excellence, however, is Yemanjá, the result of a complex syncretism. In her, pagan religions and Christianity converge, the African and Native American cultures combine with those of Europe. In Africa, Yemanjá (from the Yoruba *yeyé*, "mother," and *eya*, "fish") was the goddess of the waters, daughter of the heavens and the earth. Benevolent genetrix of all the other divinities, her womb is perennially swollen, as are her breasts, from which flow forth the rivers of the universe.

Yemanjá emigrated with the slaves from the coasts of Dahomey to the opposite shore of the Atlantic, reappearing in the African American rites of collective possession known as Santería (named also Lucumí or Yoruba) in Cuba and the Dominican Republic, Candomblé in Eastern Brazil, and Macumba in Rio de Janeiro, which then spread to other Latin American countries, including Uruguay, where the black component of society is small.

Seducer, Siren—at once charitable and dangerous, sweet and mortal —Yemanjá is bride and sister of Agangii, a sort of Triton. Fecund, absolute mother, she gave birth to Orungá who, as an adolescent overcome by his desire for her, took her by force. For this reason, it is said, Yemanjá can be spiritual or bestial, maternal or lascivious. Many believe that, together with her brother Oshalá, the highest divinity, she conceived Shangó, the irrascible god of storm and lightning; Ogún, the god of war and metals; and Ochossi of the hunt. They say that Yemanjá, with the oracle Ifá, had a daughter, Oshún the capricious, although some insist that Oshún was her younger sister to whom she gave control of rivers and copper.

The *babalawos* who guide the cults of the Cuban Santería pass down an eloquent legend of the power of Yemanjá over the other gods. This

Carybé, *Yemanjá Pregnant with all the Rivers;* detail of an immense bas-relief.
Anthropological Museum of San Paulo. Photograph by Patrizia Giancotti.

African American Siren is the adoptive mother of Shangó, who, not recognizing her at a feast, fell in love with her. Yemanjá, intent on teaching him a lesson, invited him to accompany her home. She took him by boat to the open sea where, covering him with a giant wave, she sent him to the bottom. Shangó finally managed to reach the surface again and grabbed onto the boat in panic, saying: "You who swim like a fish, save me!" Yemanjá answered that she would save him on the condition that he be more respectful toward his mother. Obatalá, his true mother, who observed the scene, added: "You must respect Yemanjá, because she is also your mother. I gave birth to you, but she brought you up. You have two mothers." This would explain the great reverence that Shangó demonstrates for both.

At any rate, the maternal aspect of Yemanjá is so overwhelming that the babalawos must take care not to err when, during the ceremony of the *asiento,* they establish the tutelary deity of the initiate. For the Siren is "greedy for sons," and capable of appropriating for herself even those belonging to other goddesses.

People who have Yemanjá as a *santo,* or personal saint, have a tendency toward grandeur, luxury, pride, and have the ability to cook well. Their rapport with the sea is highly complex: a strong fear induces them to maintain a respectful distance.

In Cuba, Yemanjá is identified with the Virgen de Regla, patron of the Port of Havana. Her feast day is on September 8, and for eight successive days, her votaries cross the bay to the village of Regla, where in 1690 the Lucumí erected the first sanctuary to her. The rites include ablutions

Tony Evora, Yemanjá; cover of the book *Yemayá y Ochún* by Lydia Cabrera, 1979. Library of Congress, New York.

on the shore, blood-shedding with slaughtered ducks, and bullfights. The Siren, with skin as black as coal, can appear either in the form of Yemanjá-Olokó, a joyous expression of the crest of the wave, constantly raising the hems of her skirts so as to move the waters, or as the fearful Yemanjá-Asezú, who drags the unfortunate to the underwater abyss.

Among the female dieties of Brazil, Yemanjá occupies the highest position. For her permanent home, the Siren chose Bahia de Sao Salvador and in particular the deep waters of the Lagoon of Abaeté at Itapoa. In that magical northeastern city her followers are countless: they wear her turquoise-colored stone around their necks as a sign of their loyalty and venerate the things that represent her, such as the shell, the smooth stone, and the round, milk-white fan *(abebé)* decorated with a Siren. They don her colors, blue and white, and pray to her, promising penance. Her adepts usually dance—trancelike—with movements imitating the waves. She is honored each year on the second day of February, the day of

Mermaid in the sand, Santa Cruz de Tenerife. Photograph by Hugo Hernandez, 1996.

Our Lady of the Rosary, in a Catholic mass that begins with the offering of the blood of two cockerels, after which terra-cotta, wood, plaster, or plastic figurines of the goddess are thrown into the water. Together with the thousands of propitiatory statuettes are baskets of flowers, letters expressing requests, and gifts appealing to her vanity: mirrors and combs, connecting her thematically with her Mediterranean incarnations, as well as soap, lipstick, and bottles of lavender perfume, her favorite. If the object remains afloat, it means that the Siren has refused to accept it. In this case, there is nothing to be done but prepare for misfortune.

In Brazil, *Sereia* (Siren) suffices to get her attention, but Yemanjá is also evoked with other names. The rowers call her Dona Janaíma; her black followers, Inaê or princess of Aioacá, the mysterious realm beyond the horizon. Senhora Maria is how she is known to her female worshippers fresh from a bath filled with sacred leaves and viscous substances such as *quiabo (Hibiscus esculentus),* their bodies totally shaved so that the spirit of Yemanjá can penetrate more easily. She comes to the names Ya, Queen of the Sea, Dandalunda, Oloshún, Macuná. Yemanjá's day is Saturday. And in Bahia her feast is simply splendid.

Jorge Amado unveils the secrets of the cult of Yemanjá in his novel *Mar Muerto* (1972), a tale of the sea, an almost incestuous love, and death. For this native of Bahia, Yemanjá's terrible aspect results from being raped by her son Orungá: as long as men of the sea are alive, she protects them and loves them. When they are dead, she desires their bodies.

> She is a mother of the water, the patroness of the sea, and thus men who live on the waves fear and love her. She punishes. She never shows herself to man, except when they die at sea. . . . The mother of the waters has long, blond hair, is nude under the waves, clothed only with her hair, as she is seen when the moon shines on the sea. Men of the land (but what can men of the land possibly know?) say that they are only moonbeams. But the sailors and boatmen laugh and say they know nothing. . . . They say that the voyage drowned seamen make with Yemanjá, above the seas, more rapidly than the fastest ship, to the Lands without End, is well worth this filthy life

on the wharf. . . . There was a time, and old men will remember, when the fury of Yemanjá was terrible. At that time, she would not play. The boats had no peace, and it was an awful life. Storms ripped over the waters. Then a *macumbeiro* said that she wanted human flesh. Children and young girls were brought as gifts to Yemanjá. The screams of the little girls given her to eat could be heard everywhere. The mothers lost their minds, and many ended up in prison. The authorities prohibited the celebration which was substituted by the procession of Jesus of the Mariners.

The spectacular public rites associated with Yemanjá are no longer exclusive to Bahia and Rio de Janeiro. In recent years, that cult has also spread to São Paulo, Brazil's densely populated and cosmopolitan city,

Statue of Yemanjá erected by the Santería community in Uruguay on the seashore of Montevideo next to the Parque Hotel on February 2, 1994. Photograph by the author.

where hundreds of thousands of her votaries gather. The cult of Yemanjá has been grafted onto the Catholic cult of the Virgin, and thus she is honored on December 8, the Feast of the Immaculate Conception.

In Uruguay, the most secular country in Latin America, where the traditional holidays of the Christian calendar have been made nonreligious (December 8: Beach Day; December 25: Family Day; Easter: Tourism Week, etc.), Macumba and Candomblé continue to acquire adepts. In 1994 on February 2, the day dedicated to Yemanjá, her followers placed her statue on the Rambla Sur of Montevideo, which is in one of the most beautiful areas of the capital. She was represented emerging from a shell, arms spread out toward the sea, offering the objects of her cult. On its base was a prayer in Lucumí and a poem "to the liquid goddess of the vortex and the transparent calm, a song drowned in the soft sweetness of the sand."

3

An Anthology of Sirens

Few creatures have undergone so many metamorphoses while remaining unaltered in their symbolical functions. Both in physical appearance and psychological qualities, the Sirens demonstrate an exceptional capacity to adapt, which is essentially the secret of their immortality. To observe this, let us follow them through time with the help of writers, poets, and artists who have recorded for us their adventures with those they encounter, shedding light on new facets and offering other keys for interpretation.

Toward the end of the fourteenth century, Jean d'Arras wrote *Melusine,* to relate "the true story of the amazing events which occurred in the noble castle of Lusignan in Poitou." Melusine is the French Siren par excellence. However, her appearance at the moment she exercises her powers is less like a fish-woman than like Delphina, the serpent-woman who sheltered Jove when Typhon cut his tendons, and to Echidna, who was a mixture of human, reptile, and goose, queen of earthquakes and object of veneration at Hierapolis. Melusine, by her mother's curse, is transformed into a serpent from the waist down. As her aquatic essence is minor, this metamorphosis occurs only on Saturday as she bathes. But to compensate, she can also enjoy her kind's earlier aerial essence, sprouting wings when the occasion requires it. Count Raymondin makes her acquaintance near a fountain of wisdom and is seduced by the beauty of her voice and her intelligence. He asks her to marry him, but she demands a promise from him as a condition.

> Swear to me on your honor never to attempt to see me on Saturday, nor to discover where I might be. And in exchange I swear to you, on the salvation of my soul, that on that day I shall do nothing to compromise your honor, but only reflect on ways to increase your prestige and fortune.

We can note that Melusine immersed herself in the animal depths of the hybrid in search of supernatural powers. Indeed, as a consequence of her Saturday disappearances, the wealth of her husband increased. Raymondin would have gone on happily respecting their pact if his brother had not convinced him to spy on his wife through the keyhole on the

Jean-Pierre Alaux, *The Bath*, 1966.

fateful day. Terrorized, Raymondin watches the metamorphosis: membraned bat's wings, wrinkled skin like that of a dragon, ungulate's hoof, silver-blue scales—the colors of the Lusignan coat of arms—and, slithering along the floor, the coils of a serpent. Raymondin, who had violated the pact, inveighs against fate. Melusine, with infinite grief, must leave him. She climbs to the top of the tower, where we return to the account of d'Arras:

> Emitting a chillingly mournful cry, she launched herself into the air, glided over the fruit grove and transformed into an enormous serpent, some five meters long. The window ledge from which she flew can still be seen, and the line of her foot is still imprinted. . . . The villagers stared upward in horror. She went three times around the town of Lusignan, crying piercingly and sobbing with the voice of a woman.

The expression "le cri de Mélusine" is used in France to describe the disconsolate sound of the hunted animal. Melusine would return during the night, secretly, to protect her children, and even to nurse the youngest, as the iconography illustrates. In popular tradition she is either idealized or vituperated: Melusine is a refined lady, an accomplished musician, a sorceress, a great transformer, or else she is an evil witch, a dark and lustful woman, and is, furthermore, the enemy of St. Louis, like her son Geoffrey de Lusignan. Is it simply by chance that Melusine acquires her powers on the old Sabbath day, like Mary and the witches? More than one author has elected as her historical counterpart Eleanor of Aquitaine, the inspiration of the troubadours, Countess of Poitou, queen of France and England, who brought to Henry II territory, wealth, and military strength, as well as the prestige of the southern civilization. She exits from center stage because of her husband's action but does not, however, allow this to prevent her from watching over her children. It is not surprising then that Richard the Lion-Hearted declared himself to be the son of Melusine/Eleanor. And in addition to this, Geoffrey de Bouillon; the counts of Toulouse, Luxembourg, and Sassenage; and the dukes of Saints-Valier, Beauvais, Saint-Gelais, Chevenon, Lansac, La Rochefoucauld, Landes, and, of course, Lusignan all have the figure of a Siren on their coats of arms.

In a more recent reading, Melusine is associated with the catastrophe of World War I by André Breton (1896–1966). Before being

Frontispiece for one of the first editions of *Melusine:* spied on by her husband at her bath, she flies away forever. Courtesy of the Forney Library, Paris.

Kiyokata Daburagi, *Yzo Gyo,* 1930, from the album of the Japanese painter. In the *Koyiki,*
the book of Shinto religion written by Yasumaro in 712, there is a legend similar to that of
Melusine: Toyo-tama-bime, daughter of the god of the sea and bride of Ho-wori, turns into
a sea monster every time she gives birth and, surprised by her husband, vanishes forever.

interrupted by man's blundering impatience, Melusine was able to exist
outside of historical time. In this liberty she represented the joie de vivre
of nature and childhood. It is war that is savage not she, not that voice
that might have spoken of love and loyalty to her companion and her
sons and remained unheeded. Melusine is the child-woman, of that species so rare that has always fascinated the poets "since time has no hold
over her."

Paracelsus (1493–1541), one of the founders of experimental medicine,
sustained that, just as the comets are monsters of the stars, and midgets

and giants are monsters produced by the union of sylphs and pygmies, the Sirens are the monsters of the interbreeding of nymphs.

> The Sirens swim for the most part on the surface of the water rather than below it, live in the manner of fish and, although not having the appearance of women, in some ways resemble them. . . . It should be remembered that the nymph who unites with a mortal man will be present at the Final Judgment because through that union she acquires a soul, and is therefore a woman, and her union with a man cannot be dissolved without her consent. If her husband takes another wife without her permission, she will reappear and kill him.

Despite the fact that Paracelsus considered the Sirens merely monstrous fish, he does deserve credit for having fashioned the name *undine* and established the character of this marine creature, whose destiny would be inextricably bound to that of the Sirens. For the Swiss alchemist, an undine is an intermediate being between human and animal, one of the elemental spirits, like the nymphs of the land, the salamanders of the fire, and the sylphs of the air. The undine resides in the water and, lacking a soul, is destined to dissolve into foam, unless a man saves her with his love. But her relationships with men are ruinous and as proof of this, Paracelsus offered a poem written in 1320 by Egenoif von Stauffenberg and obviously hearkening back to the same mythic well as Melusine, in which he related the saga of an ancestor of his who died as a result of having broken his promise to keep secret the true identity of his bride, an elemental spirit of Elba.

Drawing inspiration from Paracelsus, the Baron Friedrich de la Motte-Fouqué (1777–1843) penned a short story, "Undine." The heroine, although she has the form of a normal woman, is an aquatic spirit, destined to dissolve into nothingness. One day, the waves deposit her near the cabin of a couple of fisherfolk. They adopt her in memory of their small daughter who had disappeared mysteriously. Undine would

Arthur Rackham, illustration for the *Undine* of La Motte-Fouqué, 1909.

acquire a soul, thanks to the love of Uldbrand, a young man, but because of the continuous interference of his uncle, another elemental spirit, the union is endangered. Abandoned by Undine, Uldbrand becomes enamored of Bertholde, the true daughter of the couple. As the second matrimony is about to be celebrated, Undine, as was destined, returns to offer Uldbrand a death consonant with her aquatic essence.

> And she kissed him with a kiss of celestial sweetness, as if she would not take her lips from him, but held him very close to her, continuing to weep, as though in that weeping she would completely dissolve. And her tears penetrated the eyes of Uldbrando and invaded and drowned him in a sweet pain, until he could no longer breathe and fell softly from the arms of his love lifeless onto the pillow. "I suffocated him with tears," said Undine to the servants she encountered in the vestibule as she went out. And passing through the group, which recoiled in fear, she headed slowly toward the well.

Shifting to Anglo-Saxon terrain, it seems natural to start with the Isle of Man, the traditional dwelling place of the mermaids. In the medieval church of Zennor, we find many carvings commemorating the youths seduced by mermaids and dragged to their underwater realm. The Morrigan was believed to inhabit the swamps of Pilgar. Local legends warned men to be prudent in autumn, when storms bring mist, because the Morrigan, around All Saints Day, hangs lanterns on the willows to trick travelers into losing their way. Then she plays an enchanting tune on her cane flute, transforming them into goldfish and keeping them in still waters. Rumor has it that the Morrigan lost her magic powers when Puck, king of the elves, taught the men of the island how to exorcise her one St. John's night.

William Shakespeare (1564–1616) mentions the Sirens on at least four occasions, each time highlighting a different feature. In the famous "Sonnet 119," in which the speaker recalls the pain he felt during his lover's absence, the figure of the classical Siren weeping comes forth.

Remedios Varo, *Troubadour,* 1959. © 1998 Artists Rights Society/VEGAP, Madrid.

What potions have I drunk of Siren tears
Distill'd from limbecks foul as hell within,
Applying fears to hopes, and hopes to fears,
Still losing when I saw myself to win!

In *Hamlet,* when the queen recounts Ophelia's death to her brother, the last living image of the young woman that came to her mind was that of a mermaid.

Her clothes spread wide,
And, mermaid-like, awhile they bore her up;
Which time she chanted snatches of old lauds,
As one incapable of her own distress,
Or like a creature native and indued
Unto that element; but long it could not be
Till that her garments, heavy with their drink,
Pull'd the poor wretch from her melodious lay
To muddy death.

The Siren in *The Comedy of Errors* is the enchantress of song, of hair flowing on the water—Luciana, for whom Antipholus of Syracuse has fallen lovesick.

O, train me not, sweet mermaid, with thy note,
To drown me in thy sister's flood of tears.
Sing, siren, for thyself, and I will dote;
Spread o'er the silver waves thy golden hairs,
And as a bed I'll take them and there lie,
And in that glorious supposition think
He gains by death that hath such means to die:
Let Love, being light, be drowned if she sink!

The music of the mermaids linked to the stars is used in *A Midsummer Night's Dream* as a signal to precede Cupid's apparition, who had struck a pansy with his arrow, making it magic. This typically Shake-spearean scene played out by Oberon and Puck has inspired innumer-able illustrations.

> *My gentle Puck, come hither. Thou rememb'rest*
> *Since once I sat upon a promontory,*
> *And heard a mermaid on a dolphin's back*
> *Uttering such dulcet and harmonious breath*
> *That the rude sea grew civil at her song,*
> *And certain stars shot madly from their spheres,*
> *To hear the sea-maid's music?*

Margaret Cavendish, Duchess of Newcastle (1624?–1674), was a many-faceted, eccentric personality, adulated in learned circles at Cambridge

Robert Anning Bell, illustration for an 1895 edition of *A Midsummer Night's Dream.*

and at the court of King Charles II. She was author of philosophical
pensées, observations of experimental physics, letters, prayers, and com-
edies in which she herself acted. It is probable that she is the first woman
to write about the Sirens. Below is her poem, "The Sea-Goddess."

> *My cabinets are oyster-shells,*
> *In which I keep my orient pearls;*
> *To open them I use the tide,*
> *As keys to locks, which opens wide*
> *The oyster shells, then out I take*
> *Those orient pearls and crowns do make;*
> *And modest coral I do wear,*
> *Which blushes when it touches air.*
> *On silver waves I sit and sing,*
> *And then the fish lie listening:*
> *Then sitting on a rocky stone*
> *I comb my hair with fishes' bone;*
> *The whilst Apollo with his beams*
> *Doth dry my hair from wattery streams.*
> *His light doth glaze the waters' face,*
> *Make the large sea my looking-glass:*
> *So when I swim on waters high,*
> *I see myself as I glide by:*
> *But when the sun begins to burn,*
> *I back into my waters turn,*
> *And dive unto the bottom low:*
> *Then on my head the waters flow*
> *In curled waves and circles round,*
> *And thus with waters am I crowned.*

Sirens' link with the world beyond makes them apt companions for Peter
Pan. He, like they, straddles the worlds of daylight and dreams, of life and
death. "There were odd stories about him; as that when children died he
went part of the way with them, so that they should not be frightened."

He is a creature of the air element, as they once were, but while he possesses the gift of forgetting, they possess that of memory.

It was among Wendy's lasting regrets that all the time she was on the island she never had a civil word from one of them. When she stole softly to the edge of the lagoon she might see them by the score, especially on Marooners' Rock, where they loved to bask, combing out their hair in a lazy way that quite irritated her; or she might even swim, on tiptoe as it were, to within a yard of them, but then they saw her and dived, probably splashing her with their tails, not by accident, but intentionally.

Cover of *La Vie Parisienne,* ca. 1900. Courtesy of Curzio Lao.

Peter Pan, the Walt Disney version, 1953.

They treated all the boys in the same way, except of course Peter, who chatted with them on Marooners' Rock by the hour, and sat on their tails when they got cheeky. He gave Wendy one of their combs.

The most haunting time at which to see them is at the turn of the moon, when they utter strange wailing cries; but the lagoon is dangerous for mortals then. . . . She was often at the lagoon, however, on sunny days after rain, when the mermaids come up in extraordinary numbers to play with their bubbles. The bubbles of many colors made in rainbow water they treat as balls, hitting them gaily from one to another with their tails, and trying to keep them in the rainbow till they burst. The goals are at each end of the rainbow, and the keepers only are allowed to use their hands. Sometimes hundreds of mermaids will be playing in the lagoon at a time, and it is quite a pretty sight.

William Butler Yeats dedicates to the mermaid a succinct six-line stanza from his poem, "A Man Young and Old":

> *A mermaid found a swimming lad,*
> *Picked him for her own,*
> *Pressed her body to his body,*

Laughed; and plunging down
Forgot in cruel happiness
That even lovers drown.

In another poem, "The Song of Wandering Aengus," Yeats retells the tender story of a young fisherman who caught a magical trout.

I went out to the hazel wood,
Because a fire was in my head,
And cut and peeled a hazel wand,
And hooked a berry to a thread;
And when white moths were on the wing,
And moth-like stars were flickering out,
I dropped the berry in the stream
And caught a little silver trout.

When I had laid it on the floor
I went to blow the fire aflame,
But something rustled on the floor,
And some one called me by name:
It had become a glimmering girl
With apple blossom in her hair
Who called me by my name and ran
And faded through the brightening air.

Though I am old with wandering
Through hollow lands and hilly lands,
I will find out where she has gone,
And kiss her lips and take her hands;
And walk among long dappled grass,
And pluck till time and times are done
The silver apples of the moon,
The golden apples of the sun.

In 1915 T. S. Eliot (1888–1965), before his conversion to Christianity, wrote "The Love Song of J. Alfred Prufrock," a long poem expressing deep disenchantment. For him the mermaids are indifferent to the affairs of man. Although diverting him from thoughts about his daily existence they do not offer any answers.

> *I grow old . . . I grow old . . .*
> *I shall wear the bottoms of my trousers rolled.*
> *Shall I part my hair behind? Do I dare to eat a peach?*
> *I shall wear white flannel trousers, and walk upon the beach.*
> *I have heard the mermaids singing, each to each.*
>
> *I do not think that they will sing to me.*
>
> *I have seen them riding seaward on the waves*
> *Combing the white hair of the waves blown back*
> *When the wind blows the water white and black.*
>
> *We have lingered in the chambers of the sea*
> *By sea-girls wreathed with seaweed red and brown*
> *Till human voices wake us, and we drown.*

The most famous Siren of all is unquestionably the little mermaid of Hans Christian Andersen (1805–1875). The story told by the Danish writer offers the unusual occasion of following a Siren from infancy to adolescence. Fair, blond, and blue-eyed, like all "seafolk," she spends her life in the underwater depths and, as her father is a king, her home is in a crystal palace. Entranced by her grandmother's tales of the world beyond the sea, she is amazed that on land flowers emit perfume, that the woods are green, and that the "fish" hopping on the branches know how to sing. She can hardly wait for her fifteenth birthday when she will be permitted to rise above the surface of the sea.

When that day finally arrives, her grandmother places a garland of pearl lilies on her head and, as a symbol of her rank, attaches eight large oysters onto her tail; they hurt, but if one is to be beautiful it is sometimes necessary to suffer.

Meanwhile, on a boat, a party is in progress with music and fireworks. It is the birthday of a young, black-eyed prince. The boat sinks, and the little mermaid saves the unconscious prince. Thus, the prince does not know that it was the little mermaid who saved his life. She returns to the bottom of the sea, her sadness increasing daily because she has fallen in love. She embraces the sunken marble statue that resembles him, overcome with love and nostalgia. Then she learns something fundamental from her grandmother that will lead her eventually to negate her own species. She learns about immortal souls.

"Do men, when they are not drowned, live for ever?" she asked one day; "do they not die as we do, who live at the bottom of the sea?"

"Yes," was the grandmother's reply, "they must die like us, and their life is much shorter than ours. We live to the age of three hundred years, but, when we die, we become foam on the sea and are not allowed even to share a grave among those that are dear to us We have no immortal souls, we can never live again, and are like the green rushes which when once cut down are withered for ever. Human beings, on the contrary, have souls that continue to live when their bodies become dust, and as we rise out of the water to admire the abode of man, even so these souls ascend to glorious unknown dwellings in the skies, which we are not permitted to see."

"Why have not we immortal souls?" asked the little Mermaid. "I would willingly give up my three hundred years to be a human being for only one day, thus to become entitled to that heavenly world above."

"You must not think of that," answered her grandmother, "it is much better as it is; we live longer, and are far happier than human beings."

"So I must die, and be dashed like foam over the sea, never to rise again and hear the gentle murmur of the ocean, never again to see the beautiful flowers and the bright sun!—Tell me, dear grandmother, are there no means by which I may obtain an immortal soul?"

"No!" replied the old lady. "It is true that if thou couldest so win the affections of a human being as to become dearer to him than either father or mother; if he loved thee with all his heart, and promised, whilst the priest joined his hands with thine, to be always faithful to thee; then his soul would flow into thine, and thou wouldest become partaker of human bliss. But that can never be! for what in our eyes is the most beautiful part of our body, the tail, the inhabitants of the earth think hideous: they cannot bear it. To appear handsome to them, the body must have two clumsy props, which they call legs."

Determined to conquer the pedestrian prince and acquire an immortal soul, she flees, venturing into the terrible abyss of the witch. She glides

Harry Clark,
an illustration of the
encounter with the
witch in "The Little
Mermaid," 1916.

past repugnant octopi holding human remains and even the body of a little mermaid in their tentacles. She sees chests, sunken ships, and piles of bones that form the walls of the witch's house, whose floor is crawling with snakes. There she makes a pact with the witch: she will give her melodious voice in exchange for a philter to transform her beautiful fish tail into a pair of woman's legs. She drinks the philter on the steps of the prince's palace, and falls down in a swoon.

When the sun rose she awoke, and felt a burning pain in all her limbs, but—she saw standing close to her the object of her love, the handsome young Prince, whose coal-black eyes were fixed inquiringly upon her. Full of shame, she cast down her own, and perceived, instead of the long, fish-like tail she had hitherto borne, two slender legs; but she was quite naked, and tried in vain to cover herself with her long thick hair. The Prince asked who she was, and how she had got there: and she, in reply, smiled and gazed upon him with her bright blue eyes, for, alas! she could not speak. He then led her by the hand into the palace. She found that the witch had told her true; she felt as through she were walking on the edges of sharp swords, but she bore the pain willingly: on she passed, light as a zephyr, and all who saw her wondered at her light undulating movements.

When she entered the palace, rich clothes of muslin and silk were brought to her; she was lovelier than all who dwelt there, but she could neither speak nor sing.

The two become inseparable, but still can't communicate.

"Dost thou not love me above all others?" her eyes seemed to ask, as he pressed her fondly in his arms, and kissed her lovely brow.

"Yes," the Prince would say, "thou art dearer to me than any other, for no one is as good as thou art! Thou lovest me so much; and thou art so like a young maiden, whom I have seen but once, and may never see again. I was on board a ship, which was wrecked by a sudden tempest; the waves threw me on the shore, near a holy temple, where a number of young girls are occupied constantly with religious services. The youngest of them found me on the shore, and saved my life. I saw her only once, but her image is vividly impressed upon my memory, and her alone can I love. But she belongs to the holy temple; and thou, who resemblest her so much, has been given to me for consolation; never will we be parted!"

And the prince, who is unaware of who the little mermaid really is, when he meets the fiancée chosen for him by his parents, who is just as beautiful and virtuous as the little mermaid, with the same large blue eyes and a voice besides, is convinced that he has found the girl who saved him. Nothing remains for the little mermaid to do but fling herself into the sea; she already feels her body beginning to dissolve into foam. Then the spirits of the air, so transparent and light as to float in the air without wings, carry her away and her voice returns, more spiritual than before. However, three hundred years of good actions in the torrid and pestilent zones of the world await her, after which she will finally have her immortal soul. Andersen created this cruel fable for

Edvard Eriksen, statue of the Little Mermaid in the port of Copenhagen, 1931. Courtesy of the Danish Embassy of Rome.

children and involves his young readers, assuring them that the time of that test would be shortened or lengthened proportionally to the number of good or bad children the invisible creatures of the air found along their way.

~

Oscar Wilde (1854–1900) wrote a sentimental tale entitled "The Fisherman and His Soul" in which a fisherman puts back into the sea a mermaid with amethyst-colored eyes who had become tangled in his net, and she, grateful, returns at his call to sing him marvelous songs about the world under the sea. Yet he is not content with this: he wants her love as well. To obtain it, he must reject his human soul and cut off the shadow of his body projected on the moon. The exiled soul returns every year to the shore to tempt him to reunite with it, but the fisherman refuses every time responding: "Love is better than the things you offer me, and the little Mermaid loves me." The third year, the soul succeeds in separating him from his sea love. Too late, he realizes his error and returns to the shore to call for her.

> And the black waves came hurrying to the shore, bearing with them a burden that was whiter than silver. White as the surf it was, and like a flower it tossed on the waves. And the surf took it from the waves, and the foam took it from the surf, and the shore received it, and lying at his feet the young Fisherman saw the body of the little Mermaid. Dead at his feet it was lying.
>
> Weeping as one smitten with pain he flung himself down beside it, and he kissed the cold red of the mouth, and toyed with the wet amber of the hair. He flung himself down beside it on the sand, weeping as one trembling with joy, and in his brown arms he held it to his breast. Cold were the lips, yet he kissed them. Salt was the honey of the hair, yet he tasted it with a bitter joy. He kissed the closed eyelids, and the wild spray that lay upon their cups was less salt than his tears. . . .
>
> "Flee away," said his Soul, "for ever doth the sea come nigher, and if thou tarriest it will slay thee. Flee away, for I am afraid, seeing that

Wogeler-Worpswede, illustration for "The Fisherman and His Soul,"
Lipsia edition, 1904.

thy heart is closed against me by reason of the greatness of thy love. Flee away to a place of safety. Surely thou would not send me without a heart into another world?"

But the young Fisherman listened not to his Soul, but called on the little Mermaid and said, Love is better than wisdom, and more precious than riches, and fairer than the feet of the daughters of men. The fires cannot destroy it, nor can the waters quench it. I called thee at dawn, and thou didst come to my call.

"The moon heard thy name, yet hadst thou no heed of me. For evilly had I left thee, and to my own hurt had I wandered away. Yet ever did thy love abide with me, and ever was it strong, nor did aught prevail against it, though I have looked upon evil and looked upon good. And now that thou art dead, surely I will die with thee also."

And his Soul besought him to depart, but he would not, so great was his love. And the sea came nearer, and sought to cover him with its waves, and when he knew that the end was at hand he kissed with mad lips the cold lips of the Mermaid, and the heart that was within him brake. And as through the fullness of his love his heart did break, the Soul found an entrance and entered in, and was one with him even as before. And the sea covered the young Fisherman with its waves.

To complete the character of the physician and creator of monsters in *Doctor Moreau,* H. G. Wells (1866–1946) used erudite illustrations of bird-Sirens. A later work, the novel *The Sea Lady,* touches the rich narratological vein of a mermaid who enters the life of a family, with the tumultuous consequences that follow, told with the lightest sense of humor. The narrator writes:

Such previous landings of mermaids as have left a record, have all a flavour of doubt. Even the very circumstantial account of that Bruges sea lady, who was so clever at fancy work, gives occasion to the sceptic. I must confess that I was absolutely incredulous of such things until a year ago. But now, face to face with indisputable facts in my own immediate neighbourhood, and with my own second cousin Melville (of Seaton Carew) as the chief witness to the story, I see these old legends in a very different light.

During the family's seaside vacations, the mermaid pretends to drown, hoping to be saved and to enter into contact with the man she has chosen. Gradually, the entire family and their guests are forced to change their opinions on mermaids. For example, they learn that the type of literature appreciated in the underwater abyss is cheap modern novels, read while swaying on seaweed hammocks under the light provided by phosphorescent fish. This reading matter obviously predisposes them to approach social problems with a certain frivolity and to subordinate common sense and good intentions to passion.

In her "lodgings," the mermaid makes acquaintances among her hosts' friends. The ladies would like to know more about her, specifically how seafolk reproduce, but they do not dare ask her directly, and the mermaid does not understand their beating around the bush.

"I can't see it," [one of the ladies] said, with a gesture that asked for sympathy. "One wants to see it, one wants to *be* it. One needs to be born a mer-child."

"A mer-child?" asked the Sea Lady.

"Yes—Don't you call your little ones—?"

"What little ones?" asked the Sea Lady. She regarded them for a moment with a frank wonder, the undying wonder of the Immortals at that perpetual decay and death and replacement which is the gist of human life.

Eventually the young man in the family falls in love with the mermaid, and at the novel's end he gives up his promising career and his fiancée and disappears into the moonlit waters with her. The porter is the last to see them.

He was difficult to follow in his description of the Sea Lady. She wore her wrap, it seems, and she was "like a statue"—whatever he may have meant by that. Certainly not that she was impassive. "Only," said the porter, "she was alive." One arm was bare, I know, and her hair was down, a tossing mass of gold.

"He looked, you know, like a man who's screwed himself up.

"She had one hand holding his hair—yes, holding his hair, with her fingers in among it. . . . And when she see my face she threw her head back, laughing at me. As much as to say, 'Got 'im!' Laughed at me, she did. Bubblin' over."

I stood for a moment conceiving this extraordinary picture. Then a question occurred to me.

"Did *he* laugh?" I asked.

"God bless you, Sir—laugh! No!"

. . . Did he look back, I wonder? They swam together for a little while, the man and the sea goddess who had come for him, with the sky above them and the water about them all, warmly filled with the moonlight and the glamour of phosphorescent things. It was no time for him to think of truth, nor of the honest duties he had left behind him, as they swam together into the unknown. And of the

Glynis Johns and
Anne Crawford in
Mad about Men,
1954. Photograph
courtesy of the
National Film
Archives in London.

end I can only guess and dream. Did there come a sudden perception of infinite error, and was he drawn down, swiftly and terribly, a bubbling repentance, into those unknown deeps? Or was she tender and wonderful to the last, and did she wrap her arms about him and draw him down, down until the soft waters closed above him, down into a gentle ecstasy of death?

In *Oriental Tales,* Marguerite Yourcenar (1903–1987) traces out the portrait of "The Man Who Loved the Nereids," starting from a belief that still survives in Greece. Burned by the sun, barefoot, his clothes faded and worn, his right hand permanently extended in a gesture of begging, Panegyotis has not uttered a single word since, at eighteen, he met the blond, nude Nereid. At that time, he had been handsome, proud of his parents, who were rich farmers, and about to marry the daughter of the veterinary surgeon. Then, it was as if he had been struck by a mortal malady, against which none of the traditional exorcisms of the village had any effect. He gazes emptily but can stare at the sun without batting an eyelid and can decipher in a flower or a stone signs left by the Nereids to set an appointment with him. Having abandoned the material world, Panegyotis has entered the realm of illusions, of secret realities.

> The ancient gods and goddesses are certainly dead, and the museums hold nothing but their marble corpses. Our nymphs are more like your fairies than like the image Praxiteles has led you to conceive. But our people believe in their powers; they exist as the earth exists, as the water and the dangerous sun. Summer light becomes flesh in them, and because of this the sight of them provokes vertigo and stupor. They come out only at the tragic hour of midday; they seem immersed in the mystery of high noon. If the peasants bar the doors of their houses before lying down for their afternoon nap, it is not against the sun, it is against them; these truly fatal fairies are beautiful, naked, refreshing and nefarious as water in which one drinks the germs of fever; those who have seen them languish sweetly with apathy and desire; those who have had the temerity to

Max Klinger, *Triton and Nereid*, 1895.

approach them are struck dumb for life, because the secrets of their love must never be revealed to common mortals.

You can well imagine the scene: the patches of sunlight in the shadow of the fig trees, which is not really a shadow but a greener, softer shade of light; the young man warned by the female laughter and cries, like a hunter by the sound of beating wings; the divine young women lifting their white arms on which blond hairs caught the sun; the shadow of a leaf moving over a naked belly; a clear breast whose tip is pink and not violet; Panegyotis's kisses devouring those heads of blond hair, giving him the impression of filling his mouth with honey; his desire losing itself between those blond legs. Just as there is no love without a dazzling of the heart, there is no true voluptuousness without the startling wonder of beauty. Everything else is, at the most, a mechanical function, like hunger or thirst. To the reckless young man the Nereids opened the gates of a feminine world as different from that of the island's girls as these are different from the ewes in the herd; they made him drunk on the unknown, they made him taste the exhaustion of a miracle, they made him gaze on the evil sparks of happiness.

The Sirens would move the Sicilian Giuseppe Tomasi, Prince of Lampedusa (1896–1957), to tell one of the most fascinating stories of modern Italian literature, "Lighea" (known in English as "The Siren"). In a wretched Turin café—"a Hades of sorts, populated by the lifeless shadows of retired lieutenants, colonels, magistrates and professors"— the young journalist, Paolo Corbera of the Salina family, meets an old man with the ugliest of hands, an inveterate cigar smoker with the unpleasant habit of continuously spitting. A newspaper from their common city is the pretext for the friendship of the two Sicilians. The old man, Rosario La Ciura, is a senator and one of the greatest living Hellenists. During his youth, a Siren had removed him from time but not from place: he continued to be profoundly attached to his native island. The hybrid had shown him the synthesis of two irreconcilable worlds. One tangibly physical, including the sense of smell, the other of a spirituality so refined as to lead to metaphysical visions. Obscene and prodigious, Lighea had placed the professor in so privileged a dimension that everything else appeared banal, grotesque, vulgar. Total disenchantment is the price he paid for an enchantment that lasted his life.

"To explain myself, though, I shall have to describe my adventure to you, which I seldom do. It happened when I was that young gentleman there," and he pointed to the photograph of himself. "We must go back to 1887, a time which must seem prehistoric to you, but is not so to me. . . . I was declaiming away when suddenly I felt the edge of the boat lower, to the right, behind me, as if someone had seized it to climb on board. I turned and saw her: a smooth sixteen-year-old face emerging from the sea, two small hands gripping the gunwale. The girl smiled, a slight fold drawing aside her pale lips and showing a glimpse of sharp little white teeth like a dog's. But it was not in the least like one of those smiles you people give, which are always debased by an accessory expression, of benevolence or irony, pity, cruelty or the like; this expressed nothing but itself, that is an almost animal joy, an almost divine delight in existence. This smile was the first of the spells cast upon me, revealing paradises of forgotten serenity. From rumpled sun-coloured hair the sea-water flowed over green widely open eyes down features of childlike purity.

"Our captious reason, however predisposed, rears up before a prodigy, and when faced with one falls back on memories of the obvious; I tried, as anyone else would, to persuade myself I had met a girl out bathing, and moved carefully over above her, bent down and held out my hands to help her in. But she with astounding vigour emerged straight from the sea as far as the waist and put her arms round my neck, enwrapping me in a scent I had never smelt before, then let herself slither into the boat: beneath her groin, beneath her gluteal muscles, her body was that of a fish, covered in minute scales of blue and mother-of-pearl and ending in a forked tail which was slowly beating the bottom of the boat. She was a Siren.

"She lay on her back with head resting on crossed hands, showing with serene immodesty a delicate down under her armpits, drawn-apart breasts, perfectly shaped loins; from her arose what I have wrongly called a scent but was more a magic smell of sea, of youthful voluptuousness. We were in shade, but twenty yards away the beach lay abandoned to the sun and quivering with sensuality. My reaction was ill-hidden by my almost utter nudity.

"She spoke: and so after her smile and her smell I was submerged by the third and greatest of charms, that of voice. It was slightly guttural, veiled, reverberating with innumerable harmonies; behind the words could be sensed the lazy surf of summer seas, last spray rustling on a beach, winds passing on lunar waves. The song of the Sirens does not exist, Corbera: the music from which there is no escaping is that of their voices. . . .

"Occasionally she would come ashore with hands full of oysters and mussels, and while I laboured to open the shells with a knife she would crack them with a stone and suck in the palpitating mollusc together with shreds of shell which did not bother her.

"As I told you, Corbera, she was a beast but at the same instant also an Immortal, and it is a pity that no speech can express this synthesis continually, with such utter simplicity, as she expressed it in her own body. Not only did she show a joyousness and delicacy in the carnal act quite the opposite of dreary animal lust, but her talk had a potent immediacy which I have found since only in a few great poets. Not for nothing is she the daughter of Calliope: ignorant of all culture, unaware of all wisdom, contemptuous of any moral inhibitions, she belonged, even so, to the fountainhead of all culture, of all wisdom, of all ethics, and could express this primogenial superiority of hers in terms of rugged beauty. 'I am everything because I am simply the current of life, with its detail eliminated; I am immortal because in me every death meets, from that of the fish just now to that of Zeus, and conjoined in me they turn again into a life that is no longer individual and determined but Pan's and so free.' Then she would say: 'You are young and handsome; follow me now into the sea and you will avoid sorrow and old age; come to my dwelling beneath the high mountains of dark motionless waters where all is silence and quiet, so infused that who possesses it does not even notice it. I have loved you; and remember that when you are tired, when you can drag on no longer, you have only to lean over the sea and call me; I will always be there because I am everywhere, and your thirst for sleep will be assuaged.'"

The senator left next morning; I went to the station to see him off. He was grumpy and acid as always, but just when the train began to move his fingers reached out of the little window and grazed my head.

Next day, at dawn, came a telephone call to the newspaper from Genoa; during the night Senator La Ciura had fallen into the sea from the deck of the *Rex* as it was steaming toward Naples, and although life-boats had been launched at once the body had not been found.

In *The Skin*, Curzio Malaparte (1898–1957) composed a macabre story on the theme of the Siren, fusing chronicle and fiction. He starts with the admonition by Aeschylus from *Agamemnon:* "If conquerors respect the temples and the Gods of the conquered, they shall be saved." The action in the novel takes place after the Allied landings in southern Italy in 1943, when Malaparte was liaison officer to the Allied forces. In a mealtime conversation, he affirms that the only temples or gods that remain in a Naples ruined by war are hunger and humiliation, which its women peddle to the victors. Mrs. Flat is scandalized, and General Cork pensive. The worst, however, is still to come, with the arrival of a Siren, garnished lavishly and served at the table. To imagine her as a little girl gives the entire event an even more chilling atmosphere.

> She might have been not more than eight or ten years old, though at first sight, owing to the precocious development of her body, which was that of a grown woman, she looked fifteen. Here and there, especially about the shoulders and hips, the skin had been torn or pulpified by the process of cooking, and through the cracks and fissures a glimpse was afforded of the tender flesh, which in some places was silvery, in others golden, so that she looked as if she were clad in purple and yellow, just like Mrs. Flat....
>
> A wonderful country, Italy! I thought. What other people in the world can permit itself the luxury of offering Siren mayonnaise with a border of coral to a foreign army that has destroyed and invaded its country? Ah! It was worth losing the war just to see those American officers and that proud American woman sitting pale and horror stricken round the table of an American general, on which, in a silver tray, reposed the body of a Siren, a sea goddess!
>
> "But it's a fish!" said General Cork. "It's a first-rate fish! Malaparte says it's excellent. He knows ..."
>
> "I haven't come to Europe to be forced to eat human flesh by your friend Malaparte, or by you," said Mrs. Flat, her voice trembling with indignation. "Let's leave it to these barbarous Italians to eat children at dinner. I refuse. I am an honest American woman. I don't eat Italian children!"
>
> "That's a good idea," said General Cork, his face clearing. "We

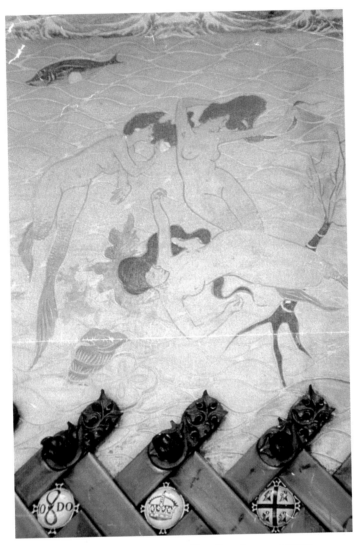

Doménech i Montaner, mural in a Barcelona restaurant.
Photograph by F. Ontañón.

can bury it in the garden." And turning to the majordomo he added:
"Please go and bury this thing . . . this poor fish in the garden.". . .

"Oh, Lord!" exclaimed Mrs. Flat, raising her eyes to heaven. She
was pale, and the tears glistened in her eyes. I was glad that she was
moved; I was deeply grateful to her for her tears. I had misjudged

her: Mrs. Flat was a woman with a heart. If she wept for a fish, it was certain that in the end, some day or other, she would also be moved to tears by the sorrows and sufferings of my own unhappy people.

In his memoirs, Pablo Neruda (1904–1973) tells of the objects collected on his travels and associated with the sea: shells, miniature ships in bottles, and figureheads.

> My biggest toys are figureheads. . . . The smallest and most delightful, which Salvador Allende so often tried to take away with him, is called Marie Celeste. She comes from an anonymous French ship which probably never sailed further than the Seine. She is cut in a dark oak, and must have sailed for many years for her to have turned forever into a mulato. She is a small woman and seems to fly with the winds, dressed in the beautiful clothing of the Second Empire. Above the dimples on her cheeks, her porcelain eyes look toward the horizon. Strange as it might seem, every year, during the winter, those eyes weep. No one can explain how or why. Perhaps the wood, as it dried out, developed some cracks which gathered water. In any case, the fact remains that those French eyes, during the winter, weep.

Rodolfo Wilcock (1919–1978), who was born in Argentina and later took Italian citizenship, wrote in both Spanish and Italian and was a rigorous translator of Shakespeare, a theater critic, and a novelist. He tells in one page the story of a Siren: victim of pollution, stripped of charisma, isolated and persecuted by men, she survives among the debris of the industrial society.

> Other sirens live in lovely underwater grottos, where orange anemones, red starfish, and brown sea urchins render the waters even more clear and blue. Gaily colored fish with the tails of tropical birds, flanks the color of precious metals. She instead is the only siren in

this wide, slimy, turbid river, living under the blackened wreck of a sunken boat, a pile of rotting wood, stuck in the mud, surrounded by rusting tin cans, bottles, greasy old shoes and repugnant, flat fish with eyes on their backs. It is even impossible to keep her hair clean. She has only one broken black plastic comb, which always catches on some filth, pieces of paper, orange peel, pieces of string which the river drags along in its enormous indifference.

So the siren is always dirty and dishevelled, and the few times she has gone to the shore to comb her hair and remove the crust of sticky mud from her scales, the local children bombard her with shards, and men make indecent proposals. One Sunday a priest even came, with three women dressed in black, waving a crucifix, to exorcize her. Thus, she decided it was wiser to stay out of sight.

The worst thing is the new chemical plant up the river, which every so often discharges irritants into the water. The siren now has a cough, and every human part of her body itches. She should really go downstream, close to the mouth of the river, but the water there is salty and unbearable to her. Upstream, the current is so strong she would have to swim all day just to remain in the same place, not even resting at night. No one cares about the solitary siren, except for a city official who every now and then comes to solicit certain family taxes which the siren has absolutely no way of paying. Thus,

Milo Manara, *The Siren;* logo for the Greenpeace campaign to curb pollution of the sea, October 1983.

what with the fertilizer factory and the taxman, the last river siren
has become very depressed and has already attempted suicide twice,
with those tubes of barbiturates which the spring floods bring.

To end this aquarium of Sirens, it would be unthinkable to omit mention of Claude Debussy (1862–1918), who presents them in musical
terms so enchanting as to induce the sense of their presence. Debussy
seems inspired by an aquatic vocation, judging by the titles of his compositions, ever allusive: *Reflections in the Water, The Submerged Cathedral,
Sails, Ondine, The Joyful Island,* for piano; *Jets of Water* and *The Tomb of
the Naiads,* based on the poetry of Baudelaire and Pierre Louÿs, respectively, for voice; *La Mer,* three symphonic sketches for orchestra: *From
Dawn to Noon on the Sea, The Play of the Waves,* and *Dialogue between
Wind and Sea.*

Who other than Debussy could have re-created the Sirens' music in
continuous metamorphosis? This he does in the third of his *Nocturnes*
for orchestra and female choir. After *Nuages* and *Fêtes, Sirènes.* Noctur-
nal Sirens, of course. Discreet bearers of Heraclitean liquescences give
the listener a gentle start. On the page, the agogic indications insist on
expressiveness *(doux, expressif, expressif et soutenu, augmentant surtout
dans l'expression),* without specifying. Female voices only, no words on
their lips, as though to confirm once more that "music begins where
words end." All the more true for the music of the Sirens.

4
Sirens and Science

Sightings, Observations, Theories

There are boatmen ferrying tourists to the Blue Grotto on Capri who claim with the most natural nonchalance that they see Sirens frequently on the rocks, combing their hair and admiring themselves in mirrors, and that the boatmen sometimes even have friendly conversations with them. There are others in Italy who believe that if they ever succeeded in hearing the Sirens' song they would become millionaires, because in it would be the winning numbers of the lottery. Sicilian seamen who have won the confidence of Sirens say that, out of the water, Sirens can only survive an hour or so, after which a bloodstain appears at the spot where they entered into the water, signaling their death. However, it is well known that ferrymen, fishermen, and seamen everywhere tend to exaggerate, often spicing up real events with images from an ancient visionary world. Be that as it may, on the topic of Sirens even the most rigorous naturalists, theologians, explorers, humanists, and scientists are apt to get excited. And despite their usual discipline and rationality, they are capable of forming the airiest of hypotheses on the widest variety of unidentified floating objects. Paradoxically, while heraldry considers Sirens "ideal figures" and does not include them in concrete situations—hunting or fishing, for example—scientists speculate about their "carnality."

Pliny, who did not believe in winged Sirens, had no trouble admitting the existence of fish-formed ones, perhaps because anomalies are extremely rare in birds, while the sea, according to the Roman naturalist, incessantly monstrifies. Women with scaled bodies known as Nereids have been heard weeping in Spanish caverns, and their corpses have been seen, swept in by the sea currents on the Portuguese coast.

St. Brendan (ca. 484–577), the Irish monk, set off with sixty companions in search of the Island of Fortune and halfway through the journey came upon a crowned Siren. His quest was recounted four centuries later in *Navigatio Brendani,* a treasure of allegorical literature. In the eighteenth century, geographical charts insisted on placing the island to the west of Ireland, later they revised this. Only the Siren, unchanged in the illustrations, seems to have had a physical reality all agreed upon.

The crusader Osbern described the "horrible voices, first soft and gentle, then as insulting laughter," which he heard when lost with his companions in a storm. There was apparently such a profusion of Sirens in the Lusitanian seas, especially during the second half of the thirteenth century, as to justify a contract between King Alfonso III and the Master of the Knights of Tiago, Paio Pérez, to put an end to the problem. In fact, it was agreed that the taxes on Sirens and similar creatures fished

Codex Palatinus Germanicus 60, Saint Brendan and his companions encounter a siren. Library of the University of Heidelberg. Courtesy of D. Lagdanovich.

off the coasts belonging to the Order would not be transferred to the Master but to the sovereign.

The *De Rerum Natura* (1249) of the Belgian Thomas de Cantimpré, although following many of the teachings of the *Liber Monstrorum,* introduced a totally new vein. Cantimpré was the first to attribute a dolphin's tail to the Sirens, rather than the usual fish's tail. He was also the first to state that they were capable of procreating and that they sometimes allow themselves to be seen nursing their children "at their large breasts on their chests."

Probably led by his desire to lend credibility to the Siren, Albertus Lucius Parvus provides many details about her, for example "long and hanging breasts" suitable for nursing, the horrible combination of flowing hair and eagle's claws, and the strangely sweet hissing that caused those hearing it to fall into a state of torpor. The Christian philosopher advises stopping up the ears and suggests another trick to make the Sirens innocuous: throwing empty bottles into the water for them to play with until the ship has safely passed.

Vincent de Beauvais (1190–1264), the Dominican confessor and protégé of Louis IX, wrote the *Speculum Majus,* one of the most impor-

Siren bearing the soul of a dead man; relief from Xanthos, Licia. Courtesy of the British Museum.

Jean de Brunhoff, Zephyr, the monkey
friend of the elephant Babar and the
mermaid Eleonore, 1936.

tant encyclopedias prior to the eighteenth century, over a twenty-four-
year period. To the jumble of anatomical details about Sirens, Beauvais
added testimonies. He tells, among other stories, of a man who, while
swimming, succeeded in capturing a Siren by grasping her by the hair.
He took her to shore and eventually even married her. Although the
man loved her, he could not bear the fact that she refused to reveal her
origins. His supplications were all in vain. Then one day, in desperation,
he threatened her with his sword, the inevitable result of which was that
the Siren returned to the sea, abandoning him forever. One must flee
from a Siren like a hare, was the Dominican's counsel.

In the 1407 Turkish romance of the Ottoman period *Iskandarname* (The book of Alexander), Ahmedi writes of a fish with a human
face and a double life: by day in water, by night on land. One is reminded
of Alexander's findings in India.

The Greek Theodorus Gaza (1398–1478), compiler of the first
grammar in his language and founder of the Academy of Ferrara in
Italy, once claimed before an audience of prominent humanists that,
following a tempest, he had seen a dying fish-woman on the sands of

the Peloponnese peninsula who quickly swam off when put back into the water.

If a prize were to be given to the place that most successfully integrated Sirens into the community, it would go to Edam, that town in the Netherlands where the following occurred. In the year 1430, after a serious flood, some girls from Edam, approaching a hill where they had left their cows, found a sea-woman stuck in the mud. They freed her, washed her, and brought her to town, where they taught her to eat bread and meat, to dress normally, to spin, and even to imitate certain gestures of Christian devotion. However, she never uttered a single word, even after they took her to Haarlem, where certain scholars attempted to teach her to speak. The Siren in question still had a strong attraction to the liquid

Joanne da Cuba, "De Piscibus," in *Hortus Sanitatis*, 1491, Magonza.

element, therefore it was necessary to remain ever alert, because otherwise she would throw herself into the nearest water.

Among the many illustrations in the first great treatise of natural history, the *Buch der Natur* (1478) of Conrad de Magenberg, there is one of a winged Siren with fish extremities and another of a nude, bicaudal Siren wearing a crown. Analogous descriptions are provided by Joanne da Cuba's chapter "De Piscibus" in the *Hortus Sanitatis* (1491) and Sebastian Brant's *Ship of Fools* (1494). The physician Guillaume Rondelet, founder of modern ichthyology, in his *Universum Piscium Historia* substantiates the representations of fish-men produced by his contemporaries, focusing in particular on the famous "monk" that "has shoulders covered with something like a monk's robe" and on the "bishop fish" with its natural miter, both armored like warriors, with scales and bony plates.

Christopher Columbus was the first to note a sighting of Sirens in the seas of the West Indies. In midocean on his return from America, at seventy-two degrees west longitude on Wednesday, January 9, 1493, in the ship's log of the *Niña,* the following is noted:

> When the Admiral reached Rio de Oro, he claimed to have seen three sirens who emerged well above the water's surface, but that they were not as beautiful as they are described as being.

The Siren of Edam; from the Zuiderzeemuseum (Museum of the Open Sea), Enkhuizen, Holland. Photograph by the author, 1996.

Some translators, attempting to improve on the accuracy of the Admiral, substitute "manatees" for "Sirens," although there is no evidence of any fables singing the praises of the beauty of those gentle, lumbering creatures. The Jesuit Charlevoix (1682–1761), in narrating the arrival of Columbus in Barcelona, adds credence to this possibility by mentioning the remains of caimans and manatees exhibited by the seamen as examples of the marvelous fauna from the New World. This did not, however, prevent Jean-Paul Clébert from taking mythical liberties with the *Niña*'s report when he recounted it:

> Christopher Columbus observed in the vicinity of Santo Domingo three Sirens dancing on the waves. However, they were not only mute but, to him, considerably unattractive, and he found that they seemed nostalgic for Greece!

King Manuel I, the Fortunate, whose reign was marked by the discovery of Brazil and the voyages of Vasco da Gama, personally attested to the existence of Sirens. He had been able to observe two surviving ones, a woman and a girl, captured in the East Indies, together with a group of Tritons. Their expression was one of profound unhappiness, and they refused to eat, losing weight visibly. The king, feeling pity for them, ordered that they be bound with a light chain and taken to the sea. Not compelled to rise to the surface for air, they dove and played underwater with such joy that it was decided to bring them there every day. By these means, their captors managed to keep them alive for a few years in the new country. These Sirens too never uttered a single word in their captivity. No one has ever explained whether they lost their voices because they were forced to live in a world unnatural to them or whether they refused to speak to avoid communicating with the inhabitants of the land.

Like Manuel the Fortunate, the Spanish kings Charles V and his son Phillip II, the Prudent, were also said to have had the privilege of observing Sirens in the flesh. Andrea Vesalio, personal physician to Charles V, presented a specimen to select circles in Amsterdam and Antwerp during the first half of the sixteenth century. Because he was one of the first

Theodore de Bry, *Americae pars quarta,* Christopher Columbus meets three Sirens in the new world; from *The Book of Navigation,* Riuniti Editions, Rome.

anatomists to have dissected the human body for scientific purposes, the Flemish physician would have been able to formulate an authoritative judgment on these examples, but he is not known to have commented on the subject.

In a text enriched by the accuracy of its illustrations, the Swiss physician Conrad Gessner relates that in 1523, in the port of Ripa Maggiore in Rome, a creature the size of a five-year-old child was captured with a horn on its forehead, webbed lower limbs, and a twin-forked fish tail. Of the same epoch is the famous "Monster of Ravenna": a bird-fish hybrid, the physical existence of which was substantiated by the most illustrious scientists of the time. Born after the bloody battle between the armies of Julius II and Louis XII, the remarkable creature had a horn, two wings instead of arms, both female and male infantile genitals, lower limbs fused into a single-scaled paw, a third eye on its knee, and the claws of a bird of prey.

In Basel, the Alsatian Jesuit Corradus Lycosthènes published the *Prodigiorum Ac Ostentorum Chronicon* in 1577. Its frontispiece illustrates, among the principle phenomena of the sky and earth, a pair of human/marine mammal hybrids. That celebrated sighting occurred in Egypt during the nineteenth year of the reign of Mauritius Tiberius, around A.D. 601 It was confirmed by the Prefect Menas, who happened at that time to be on the coast of the Delta. The male carefully kept the lower part of his body immersed in the water as though he were ashamed. The female, beautiful in form, with adolescent breasts, delicate facial features, black hair falling lightly over her shoulders, hid the rest of her body—"mysteries of the marriage bed"—in the river. Spellbound by this spectacle, the prefect, his court, and the gathered crowd remained there until sunset, when the extraordinary couple silently sank under the water.

The Monster of Ravenna, woodcut, ca. 1520.

The Nile couple, from the frontispiece of Lycosthènes' *Prodigiorum Ac Ostentorum Chronicon*, 1557, Basel.

Lycosthènes, however, is an author held in scant consideration and dismissed by the erudite for being frivolous. His style appears, to say the least, naive. Nonetheless, a few years later, the rigorous French surgeon, Ambroise Paré, reconsiders the event in his treatise *On Monsters, Both Terrestrial and Marine, and Their Portraits*. From that point on, anyone mentioning this Monster would no longer be an easy target for criticism. Was it not Paré himself who referred to the Monster of Ravenna as an "example of the wrath of God"?

Ulisse Aldrovandi (1522–1655), physician and naturalist of Bologna, called on draftsmen to translate into images the marine studies of the French naturalist Guillaume Rondelet. The resulting scientific illustrations, which were to have widespread success, included the marine couple seen on the Nile and a carp with a human face that Aldrovandi himself had caught fishing in 1585 near Retz in Austria. Finally, Athanasius Kircher,

The Nile couple, from Ulisse Aldrovandi's *Historia Monstrorum*, 1642.

writing in the mid-seventeenth century on animal magnetism, alluded to anthropomorphic fish and the miraculous effect they had, when ground into powder, on persistent hemorrhage.

The navigator Henry Hudson, on June 13, 1608, solemnly logged the testimonies of two of his crew while sailing in the warm waters of the Sea of Kara, off the east coast of New Zemlya, on an expedition to find a direct route to China through Arctic seas. The men, looking toward the North Cape, saw a mermaid. Hudson notes that she was a woman on her top half—tall, full-breasted and white-skinnned with long dark tresses. When she dove, her dolphin's tail could be seen, blue-green with black stripes.

Captain John Schmidt described a Siren with a beautiful mass of long hair encountered near the Canadian port of St. John in 1610. With an insistence inappropriate in the gentle sex, she tried at all costs to come on board. He and his crew, however, terrorized, staved her off, striking

Fish woman sighted by the Spanish in the seas of the West Indies, from *Essais de la nature qui apprend a faire l'homme* by Jean-Baptiste Robinet, 1768.

her with canes and sticks until she disappeared once more below the waters. In his book on those "forsaken by God," Martin Monestier attributes the following comment to the captain: "A Siren of great beauty, hair of a blue cast falling over white shoulders, pear-shaped breasts, and a sensual smile."

The Benedictine monk Benito Jeronimo Feijóo (1676–1764), author of *Teatro Crítico Universal,* a much-consulted encyclopedia of its time, reformulated an opinion already contested by Aristotle and Lucretius: "We could suppose that they were the result of the perverse coitus of individuals of the two species." Perhaps this could explain why, in Spain, seamen and fishermen were obliged to swear before a magistrate that they would abstain from having carnal intercourse with Sirens if they should encounter them. Notarial documents of this type were still being drawn up as late as the mid-nineteenth century.

In an Indonesian publication dated 1717 there is a detailed account of the capture off the Borneo coasts of a "widow of the sea." Fifty-nine inches long and as thick as an eel, it lived for four days and seven hours in a water tank. Every now and then it let out short squeaks similar to those of a rat. It refused the food it was offered and left excrement similar to that of a cat.

Among the astonishing results in natural and kabbalistic magic described by Albertus Lucius Parvus—various French versions of whose work circulated during the eighteenth century—is the bird-Siren obtained by means of what could be considered an early experiment in genetic engineering. He tells how an anonymous Jew from Metz used a recipe taken from Avicenna (980–1037) to produce a demonlike being defined as a "mandrake." So small as to fit in the palm of the hand, it had the body of a guinea hen and the face of a young girl. The creature, which proved to be very obliging toward its master, procured him incalculable wealth. The following are the instructions of "Petit Albert":

Take a large egg of a black hen, prick it, and extract some of the white, in the amount equivalent to a broad bean. After having filled it with human semen, close the orifice lightly, with a fragment of

Mandrake-siren created in the sixteenth century using a recipe of Avicenna's; from *Libellus de mirabilus Naturae arcani* by Albertus Parvus, Lyon edition, end of the eighteenth century.

moistened parchment. Allow it to incubate then for the first day of the March moon in a fortunate constellation of Mercury and Jove. At the end of the necessary period, the egg will crack, freeing the little monster you see here, which must be nourished in a secret room with lavender seeds and worms. What you see in the wood-engraving lived just one month and five days. Should you wish to preserve it after its death, place it in a heavy glass jar with wine spirits and close tightly.

Discoveries in the British territories have been countless. We know that in 1814, near Belfast, an Irish fisherman named William Dillon caught a mermaid in his net. She measured five feet four inches, tail included. Her mouth was large, her nose turned up, her hair long and green. Shortly afterward, the English newspapers reported the sighting of another very beautiful Siren with aristocratic grace, in Sandside, in the Scottish county of Caithness. Before returning underwater, she allowed the large crowd to admire her nude body for about an hour. As recently as 1961 a tourist office on the Isle of Man offered a prize to anyone who caught a living Siren in the local waters.

Turning to the Arctic seas we find, according to eyewitnesses, the Sdivonites, human-cetacean hybrids that settled in the double-bottomed, interconnecting lakes described in certain reports of polar expeditions. Monestier reported that some members of the 1823 Weddell Expedition to the Antarctic claimed to have seen women with green hair, attractive enough from the waist up, but with the rest of their bodies similar to seals. One very interesting detail: they sang melodies resembling hymns.

In 1560 on the eastern coast of Ceylon, near the island of Manar, Portuguese fishermen reported catching nine Sirens and seven Tritons in a single net. Performing the autopsy on them was none other than the Viceroy of Goa. The scientists and Jesuits present claimed not to have observed any anomalies in their anatomies, which were similar to humans'. In Ceylon, again, at the end of the eighteenth century, one Reverend Henriquez relates that he was called to baptize eleven marine creatures and that the opinions expressed as to the appropriateness of conferring the sacrament in that case were conflicting. On the coast of Sumatra, a Siren was found by a group of Malaysians and then sold

Embalmed Siren, actually a combination of the upper half of a monkey and the lower half of a fish. Venice Museum of Natural History. Photograph by Enzo Ruffert.

"Living Bird Woman," attraction in an American circus at the end of the nineteenth century, Paris. Courtesy of the Musee de l'Affiche, Paris.

and exhibited in London in 1832 as a sideshow attraction. However, the attentive eye of scientists revealed it as a fake, being composed of the upper part of a female monkey and the lower part of a tuna.

Though the bird-woman, as a result of various degrees of trickery, has often been present in sideshows, the major attraction has always been the fish-woman. A notable example of this was the "fascinating fish woman" or "living mermaid" presented to the public in the mid-nineteenth century by P. T. Barnum. However, ticket bought and paid for, what the disappointed spectator actually saw was sixty centimeters of a clever, stuffed imitation. It was said to have been authenticated by reputable scientists as native of the Fiji Islands, which were at that time the last stronghold of cannibalism.

Three works of sesquipedalian title were the source of much of the information provided: *Telliamed ou Entretiens d'un philosophe indien avec un missionnaire français, sur la diminution de la mer* by Benoit de

Maillet (The Hague, 1745); *Vue philosophique de la gradation naturelle des formes de l'être, les essais de la nature qui apprend à faire l'homme* by Jean-Baptiste Robinet (Amsterdam, 1768); and *Sirènes, Essai sur les principaux mythes relatifs à l'incantation, les enchanteurs, la musique magique, le chant du cigne* by Georges Kastner (Paris, 1858). The *Telliamed* (which is an anagram of the author's name), written a good hundred and thirty years before Darwin, contains hints of animal transformations that could be considered precursors of the theory of evolution. In it, Maillet de Lorraine—consul to Louis XIV in Egypt, Ethiopia, and Italy—maintains that the sea, after once covering the entire globe, subsequently shrunk; thus all living beings are descended from aquatic creatures. Detailed documents tending to confirm this thesis alternate with purely imaginary accounts. Although Voltaire considered Maillet *un pen blessé du cerveau*, the *Telliamed* provided material for the more or less scientific writings of numerous scholars, from the Enlightenment to the present. Robinet's book proceeds in the same direction, every case supported by graphic representations. The third, defined by the author as a "book/musical score," in addition to providing numerous accounts, is illustrated with finely

Poster for the Barnum & Bailey Circus, end of the nineteenth century. In its center is "a living mermaid."

detailed lithographs and at the end includes a musical score for solo voice, choir, and orchestra.

A singular theory has been advanced on sightings of these wondrous sea creatures by Canadian scientists. With the aid of a computer, they concluded that a large cetacean, distorted optically by the atmospheric conditions preceding a storm, could appear to be a phantasmagoric animal. The increasing rarity of these mirages might be attributed to the change in position of the observer on ships, sitting progressively higher on the water, or to the declining numbers of cetaceans themselves.

Rather than attempting to determine whether the Sirens are concrete objects distorted by erroneous perception or abstract figures created entirely by the imagination, we might do well to think of them as a symbol. A symbol of unfathomable depth that persists with rare tenacity, proof of the force of the psychic event that created them.

Physical and Psychic Anomalies

The prejudices that have surrounded monsters over the centuries are well known. While it is true that the ancient Egyptians admitted them to their necropolises, honoring them as sacred animals, elsewhere, more often than not, they were considered signs of diabolical possession or the result of perverse, human coupling with beasts. During the Middle Ages, the serious problem presented by monsters certainly contributed to the obscuring of the ancient luminescence of the Sirens. Even in the eighteenth century, a woman could be condemned to the stake for giving birth to an infant with catlike features; that fact is referred to without the slightest indignation by Bartolini, a member of the illustrious Scandinavian family of physicians and scientists.

One of the malformations studied by teratology is sirenomelia, a rare birth defect in which an infant is born with limbs like a Siren. The first case of sirenomelia recorded was the "parturition on Bourbon soil" of an infant who survived for only an hour. The child's lower limbs were fused into a single tail-like form at the extremity of which was a foot. Sereniform fetuses are known as *Sirenomelia mono podica, cuspidata, simmelia, simpodia,* or *meloateplasia,* according to the way the lower part of the body is formed. Usually they have only one fibula and lack an external outlet for the digestive, genital, and urinary systems. From the rudimentary ovaries examined during autopsies it has been possible to determine that affected infants are usually female.

In the infinite range of the psychological anomalies, there is a curious fixation linked to the Sirens, which was identified and explored by the English physician Havelock Ellis (1859–1939). Since one of his patients suffering from this affliction was called the "fairy of the waters" or "spirit of Nature" by those who knew her, Ellis decided to name the phenomenon ondinism. This condition, which Ellis argues is related to excessive childhood bedwetting, makes it impossible to experience sexual pleasure without urinating. Ellis believes that the tendency to take an interest in the act of urination, which he claims is particular to women and priests, harkens back to our saltwater animal ancestors and our own embryonic state in which the bladder is almost inseparable from our environment. The bladder retains psychic associations with rain, sacred

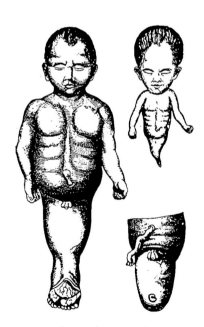

Cases of sirenomelia.

waters, and legends of the great flood. Considering the quantity of such symbols, Ellis believes the vesical psychic life may be even more active and interesting than the sexual one.

Sirens and Zoology

It is considered "rational" or "scientific" to assume that Sirens resulted from the mistaken perceptions or wishful thinking of sailors, during long periods of imposed abstinence, upon seeing a female sea mammal about sixteen feet long with breasts high on the upper part of its body. The euhemerists felt it necessary to bring the phenomenon back into the "natural" order of things. The long hair they comb? Nothing more than seaweed. The melancholy face of a woman? The muzzle of a manatee or seal. And the irresistible song leading to forgetfulness? Only air whistling through holes, waves breaking on the rocks. And thus, they state triumphantly, is the mystery of the Sirens resolved.

On this premise, we need to list briefly the marine mammals who have earned the name of Sirenians—herbivores, cataloged in the nineteenth century under the scientific name of *Siren sirenidae.*

Ritines—a family that was totally extinct by the eighteenth century due to uncontrolled hunting; inhabited the Bering Sea.

Dugongs or sea cows—found in the Indian Ocean, Australia, the Persian Gulf, and the Red Sea; have been known since ancient times by the Jews and were initially called *Dugon tabernaculi* because their durable skin was used to cover the Ark of the Covenant. Compared to cetaceans because of their fins, they have bilobate tails and bodies some ten feet long. They live in coastal waters, graze on underwater grasses, and are much appreciated for their skins, fat, and meat, which has a sweet taste.

Manatees—from the Caribbean, Florida, and the Amazon, they frequent the coastal zones and estuaries. Their divided upper lips are prehensile and are used to gather aquatic plants for food.

The Sirenians differ from other cetaceans in their squat head, flat muzzle, tactile bristles on the upper lip, and rigid eyelids with small eyes, whose continuous secretion of mucilage can give the impression of tears. They also have well-articulated pectoral fins, round mammary glands on the front of their bodies, a rounded caudal fin positioned transversally, and thick skin. Their most probable ancestor is the elephant, which lost its posterior limbs once it adapted to the sea. They reproduce once every two or three years. The females have ventral genital organs, very similar to those of a woman. At fifteen-minute intervals, they come to the surface for air. Their cries are guttural. While water pollution destroys their sources of food, scars on their backs from boat propellers have become progressively more common. They, like the Sirens, are victims of humankind's myopia and deafness.

In 1982 a large group of scientists from the various branches of biology founded the International Society of Cryptozoology, chaired by Bernard Heuvelmans. With headquarters in Tucson, Arizona, the Society is concerned with the possible presence—past or present—of animals in areas where their existence had been unknown as well as the survival of species previously presumed extinct. The objects of their investigations include

Manatee. Photograph by James A. Sugar, courtesy of the National Geographic Society, 1984.

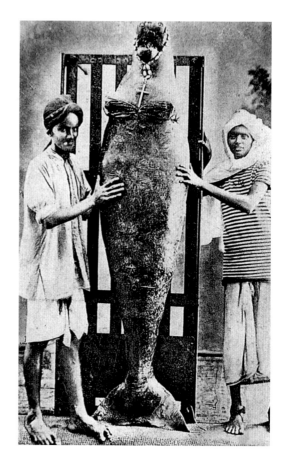

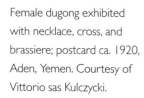

Female dugong exhibited with necklace, cross, and brassiere; postcard ca. 1920, Aden, Yemen. Courtesy of Vittorio sas Kulczycki.

zoological enigmas such as the Yeti, sea serpents, the Loch Ness Monster, the varanid of the Fiji Islands, and the four species of cetaceans of which only a single example has been found in recent decades. Heuvelmans himself says that, given the ignorance of science regarding the marine environment, no possibility should be excluded when dealing with that element. Consequently, should the announcement be made tomorrow of the capture of a Siren, with the face and torso of a beautiful woman and the tail of a fish, a scientist expressing the desire to see her would be more responsible than one who received the news with a shrug of the shoulders.

In the end, the Sirens may lie outside the sphere of the natural sciences. Neither monsters nor beasts, far less women halved, they are symbols once more.

5
Modern Sirens

Sirens in Pop Culture

By now we can all describe them, so rooted are they as a figurative motif in contemporary culture. The bicaudal Sirens—the obsession of Romanesque churches and heraldry—are endangered. The single-tailed Sirens have triumphed, incontestable and radiant feminine beauties with their pisciform parts created by innumerable contrivances.

Sirens appear tattooed on the backs and biceps of sailors. Sirens drip water from fountains. Refined Sirens parade in Lalique crystal, in pre-Raphaelite paintings, in Art Nouveau furnishings, in fairy-tale illustrations. Sirens star in film, on mannered and pop postcards, on Siren-shaped forks, lampshades, and keychains.

Nothing seems more normal than the advertising techniques that use the image of Sirens to seduce, enchant, attract. Subjugated to the cause of commerce in seaside lido signs and gymnasium and swimming pool emblems, Sirens also appear as signs for aquatic amusement parks

Miniature plastic mermaids used as party decorations, 1992, Denmark. Courtesy of Fanchita González Battle.

Silver saltcellar with green stone by Henri Nocq, 1890, Paris. Photograph by Paul Louis.

Sculpted table by G. Mario Confente, from "Furniture Arcade" in the magazine Amica Casa, May 27, 1995.

Left: "Mostacciolo," traditional honey cookie of Calabria

Right: Fishhook with plastic mermaid as bait, 1950, United States.

Three sirens in three decades of cinema: Ann Blyth in *Mr. Peabody and the Mermaid,* 1948; Glynis Johns in *Mad about Men,* 1954; and Dominique Bosquero in *Mare Matto* (Crazy Sea), 1963. Courtesy of the archives of M. Gustin.

offering the spectacle of trained whales and dolphins. In serving the interest of the exploiters of beach, shellfish, or mineral water, Sirens have preserved their ancient link with the liquid element. Advertising grasps their wondrous allure, as undeniable as ever.

These Sirens no longer divert but lead us along the road to consumption. No longer chanting melodies, they hawk products. Mute and beckoning, they join the fray. In their mirror, we see not our own depths but our magnified ego.

Now to announce a product is not enough; like the Sirens, it must galvanize the attention of the public. This not-so-subtle art of persuasion draws considerable advantage from the magic chant, knowing that even the most banal message can acquire a power to penetrate and persuade when accompanied by propitious sound.

From Myth to Mechanism

In 1818 French physicist Cagniard de Latour gave the name siren to a measuring device he invented to determine underwater sound vibrations resulting from interruptions in the liquid current. But there exists an apparatus much more modest in scope that has a far greater right to use the same name. This is the mechanical siren invented by Hooke in 1700; improved by Savart in 1830, Seebreck in 1841, and Koefling in 1881; and perfected in an electromagnetic version by Weber in 1885. It consists of motor-driven rotating disks that, by forcing air toward a series of perforations, produce intense and prolonged acoustic signals or alarms.

Each of us encounters these sirens, indiscriminating, now determined to reach every ear. And how they have changed from their mythical ancestors. Physical vibrations, no longer complex creatures. Piercing mechanical wails, no longer enticing, extraordinary voices. Sound, not song. And their homes are now congested urban landscapes, no longer fresh, seaside places. However, all the deafening hissing that suddenly invades the city is really no more than the terminal point of the long road that began with the arcane musical message of the *Odyssey*. In fact, the Sirens continue to challenge man's "deafness," overcoming his sense

Italian advertisement for
"Blue Ribbon" beer, 1995.

"Magic Mermaid Barbie";
cover of a school notebook, 1993.

of hearing, the sense of his place in space and time. They want us to pause, observe, become aware of the situation, reflect for an instant, and if possible turn away from the path we have taken.

The experts teach us that there is an active way of listening, as if we were under the spell of Pan, not only concerned with the recognizable sound, or the individual speaking, but with deciphering the speaker's inadvertent messages and our own inner ones. Listening and accepting the risk of being captured by the other. Listening precisely as the Sirens have always demanded, whatever their momentary form.

The Sirens rise up once more. And although it is man who arbitrates their sound, rendering it uniform, it nonetheless proceeds in Pythagorean intervals, as if conjecturing the past. Although no longer the exceptional event, they are its call. Although governed by technology, they continue to officiate at a passage. And the ambulance, fire department, and police vehicles, which move to the sound of howling sirens and enjoy absolute priority in city traffic, are also there to indicate that someone is on the threshold of a transit, someone is at the point of changing, someone may cease to be what he or she is.

All the languages in the world have preserved intact this ancient lesson, giving the same name—Siren—to both the Homeric seductresses and the noisy device. In his *Bestiaire,* Apollinaire emphasizes the dual nature of the term in the following quatrain:

How should I know, Sirens, where your tedium comes
    from
When you moan in the night from far off the shores?
Sea, like you, I'm full of scheming voices
And my singing ships are called my years.

Although they may be encapsulated and reduced to mere mechanisms, the Sirens are still intent on communicating basic truths: this is perhaps their way of remaining immortal. And each time they sound, time seems to stand still, to help us understand the permanent significance of their message.

Man, however, creates his gods in his own image and likeness, and if we judge him on his treatment of the Sirens, contemporary man's thirst for knowledge, as compared to his Homeric ancestors, seems somewhat limited. He wants to know that his property is not threatened. Thus, the sirens most dear to him are burglar or car alarms. That disturbing howl more often than not turns out to be a false alarm. Someone, distracted, neglected to read the instructions carefully, or else a stray cat has nudged against the fender of someone's car. The system is imperfect because too perfect, defective because it is too sophisticated. We no lon-

Poster for Riccione, "the green pearl of the Adriatic," 1925, Argo Press, Bologna. From the collection of the author.

ger need to stop up our ears with wax or have ourselves bound to the mast, for the danger of fatal allure is nonexistent. The security company arrives; public peace of mind must not be disturbed. "The siren has been deactivated," the security man announces, soothing all tempers. Well controlled by man, it is clear that these sirens will not be persecuted as their mythical sisters were. And this comes as no surprise in times when the desire for silence is considered an eccentricity.

The most powerful siren in history, tuned to "A" as finely as a symphony orchestra instrument, is that of the ocean liner *Queen Elizabeth*. A mysterious gravity settles on us at the sound of ship sirens announcing their presence as their routes cross on the open sea. Albert Camus (1913–1960) offers some surprising associations.

"Don't accept Levi's from strangers"; Roman billboard, May 1992. Photograph by the author.

In the afternoon, we crossed with a steamship heading in the direction of the city. The greetings exchanged by the sirens were like three loud yelps of prehistoric animals, the signs of passengers lost on the sea and stimulated by the presence of other men, the distance between the two ships increasing slowly up until the final separation in unfriendly waters.

The sound of sirens awakens associations with bellowing, howling, roaring, hissing, whining, barking—an obscure and frightening animal to be exorcised. It is incomprehensible sound emitted by the wounded, choleric, or desperate beast, deprived of its territory, caged in by technology, prevented from flying or swimming, magic stolen. The lament of the mourning Sirens, the lacerating scream of Melusine. A howl suffocated in a bewildered throat; rootless voice, body amputated from its human nature, human nature amputated of its female parts. A new hybrid emerges: a monstrous crossbreed between an organ of phonation and a machine.

Sirens are the deforming mirror, changing screen, containing every possible metamorphosis, fulmination. They speak of death to a civilization that would prefer to ignore it, one that denies their initiatory powers. The winged figures startle with their call. The sudden sonorous

Make way for the siren! postcard, Beatrice d'Este Editions, Graphic Art Memories, Milan, 1978.

arrival of sirens causes a sense of premonition, of threat, provoking that ancestral emotion that triggers chemical reactions and accelerates the heartbeat. They act upon our primitive reptile brain, echoing our own hybrid within, our oldest fear of the claw that slashes or the teeth that drag us into the abyss of the sea. Ensnared by this arcane power, we are pervaded by an obscure sense of dissolution, dismayed and seized by a compulsion to flee.

In the past: fear and fascination. In the present: fear only. In the past, a leap into the sea, into darkness, the unknown. Today the alarm, *la larme:* the tear—essence of human affliction, certainly, but also of

Hood ornament on the Dupont
Royal Town Car G, 1930.

Advertisement for Aqua Dry,
a wet/dry vacuum, in *L'Espresso*,
December 1980, Rome.

boundless joy. The Sirens continue to express themselves through oxymoron. Tear: drop of salty liquid, ultimately. How well José Durand wrote:

> The siren is salt. Inseparable, intimate nature of the seas. Without which it would be tasteless. It is death and life. Sowing salt—the extreme ignominy—is equivalent to sowing death. When salt is lacking—or else, if death is lacking—no life is possible. Salt reigns, the siren reigns, source of grace. Salt and the siren are life and death, and hence, dream.

Dream, symbol. We could then say that today's sirens are the reemergence of the weeping, hair-tearing, breast-beating tomb Sirens of Greece. Or of those forces who, with a cosmic music, procure the pleasure of death. They are the inextricable presence of distant and coeval events, of the real and the phantasmagoric. The last metamorphosis of the Sirens, their last face in history. And our last rejection of them.

Still ambivalent then, indicating both the alarm and the all clear, Sirens have learned to rise above the feral howling created by man. Since the first World War, perched atop churches and city towers, they have been warning of the arrival of a new breed of death-bearing birds. In the event of disaster, sirens start automatically. Could that be the only way they have left to continue their chant, whatever it may be, in the stubborn hope that someone might listen?

John William Waterhouse, *A Mermaid*, 1900.

Bibliography

Aeschilus. *Le Tragedie: Prometeo incatenato.* Bologna: Il Mulino, 1965.

Aethenaeus. *Orphicum Fragmenta.* Selected by O. Kern. Berlin: n.p., 1963.

Albertus Lucius Parvus. *Libellus de mirabilus Naturae arcanis.* Lyon: n.p., 1791.

Alciati. *Emblemata.* Lyon: Guillaume Rouille Librairie, 1548.

Aldrovandi, Ulisse. *Monstrorum historia.* Bologna: n.p., 1642.

Alighieri, Dante. "Inferno" XIII, 13; "Purgatorio" XIX, 20 and XXXI, 44; "Paradiso" XII, 6. In *La Divina Commedia.* Florence: Ed. La Nuova Italia, 1957.

Amado, Jorge. *Mar morto.* Rio de Janeiro: Editora Record, 1980.

Anacreon. *Antologia della Lirica Greca.* Rome: Ed. Valmigli, 1954.

Andberg, Bjarne. "Le paysage marin dans la crypte de la cathédrale d'Anagni." In *Acta ad Archaeologiam et artium pertinentia.* Rome: Istituto Norvegese, 1965.

Andersen, Hans Christian. *Fairy Tales and Legends by Hans Andersen.* London: The Bodley Head, 1935.

Apollinaire, Guillaume. *Alcools.* "Lul de Fantenin," translated by Jon Graham. Paris: Mercure de France, 1913.

———. *Le Bestiaire ou Cortège d'Orphée.* Translated by Lauren Shakely. New York: The Metropolitan Museum, 1911.

———. *Selected Poems.* Translated by Oliver Bernard. London: Penguin, 1995.

Apollodorus. *Bibliotheca* I, 33-4-9-25.

Apollonius of Rhodes. *Argonautica,* Book IV. Translated by R. C. Seaton. Cambridge: Harvard University Press, 1912.

Aristotle. *Metaphisica I.* Uncatalogued manuscript.

———. *History of Animals.* London: Adamant Media Corp., 2005.

Aristotle, Pseudo. *De mirabilis auscultationibus,* cap. 110.

Arras, Jean d'. *Mélusine.* Edited by Michèle Perret. Paris: Editions Stock, 1979.

Augustine, Aurelius. *La città di Dio,* Book XVI, cap. 8. Edited by M. C. Borgogno.

———. *De beata vita, I,* 1–4. Rome: Edizioni Paoline, 1963.

Bachelard, Gaston. *Water and Dreams: An Essay on the Imagination of Matter.* Translated by Edith R. Farrell. Dallas: Pegasus Foundation, 1983.

Bachofen, Johan Jakob. *Introduction to Mother Right.* Rome: Editori Riuniti, 1983.

Baer Eva. *Sphinxes and Harpies in Medieval Islamic Art: An Iconographical Study.* Israel: The Israel Oriental Society, 1965.

Baltrusaïtis, Jurgis. *Il Medioevo fantastico.* Milan: Mondadori, 1977.

———. *Réveil et prodiges: le Gotique fantastique.* Paris: Armand Collin, 1960.

Barb, Alphonse A. "Antaura, the Mermaid and the Devil's Grandmother." In *Journal of the Warburg Institute,* vol. 29. London: n.p., 1966.

Barnum, Phineus T. *Struggles and Triumphs.* Salem, N.H.: Ayer, 1970.

Barrie, James Matthew. *Peter Pan.* 1911; reprint, New York: Viking, 1991.

Baudelaire, Charles. *Les fleurs du mal.* Edited by G. Chesters. United Kingdom: Duckworth Pr. Ltd., 1988.

Baudrillard, Jean. *De la séduction.* Bologna: Cappelli, 1981.

De Beauvoir, Simone. *The Second Sex.* Translated by H. M. Parshley. New York: Knopf, 1953.

Bestiaire of Cambridge, II, 4, 26. Oxford: Cambridge University Library, 1928.

Blanchot, Maurice. *Le livre à venir.* Turin: Einaudi, 1969.

Boccaccio, Giovanni. *L'Ameto o Commedia delle Ninfe fiorentine.* Riccardo Ricciardi Editore, 1952.

Bolen, Jean S. *Goddesses in Everywoman: A New Psychology of Women.* San Francisco: HarperCollins, 1985.

Bologna, Corrado. *Liber Monstrorum de diversis generibus, libro deile Miravili difformitá.* Milan: Bompiani, 1977.

Bonnefoy, Yves. *Dictionnaire des Mythologies.* Paris: Flammarion, 1981.

Borges, Jorge Luis, and Margarita Guerrero. *Manual de zoología fantástica.* Mexico: Fondo de Cultura Económica, 1957.

Bowra, Maurice. *The Romantic Imagination.* New York: Oxford University Press, 1950.

Bravetta, Ettore. *La leggenda del mare e le superstizioni dei marinai.* Palermo: Il Vespro, 1979.

Breton, André. *Arcane 17 Enté d'Ajours.* Paris: Ed. du Sagittaire, 1947.

Bril, Jacques. *Lilith ou La Mère obscure.* Paris: Payot, 1981.

Browning, Robert. "The Englishman in Italy." In *The Complete Works of Robert Browning,* vol. IV. Athens, Oh.: Ohio University Press, 1974.

Brückner, Aleksander. *Mitologia slava.* Bologna: Zanichelli, 1923.

Buffiere, Félix. *Les mythes d'Homère et la pensée grecque.* Paris: Soc. Edit. Les Belles Lettres, 1973.

Cahier, Charles, and Arthur Martin. *Mélanges d'Archéologie*. T. II, Bestiaires. Paris: Poussielgue-Rusand, 1851.

Calderon de la Barca. *Comedias*. Vol. II, *El Golfo de las Sirenas*. Madrid: Rivadeneyra Editor, 1881.

Camara Cascudo, Luis da. *Dicionário do folklore brasileiro*. Rio de Janeiro: Instituto Nacional do Livro, Ministerio Educaçao e Cultura, 1962.

Campbell, Joseph. *The Hero with a Thousand Faces*. Princeton, N.J.: Princeton University Press, 1972.

Candea, Virgil, and Constantin Simionescu. *Rumanische Kulturpräsenzen*. Jerusalem: Dieselbe Handschrift Tierkreisbuch, n.d.

Canselier, Eugène, disciple of Fulcanelli. *Mutus Liber: L'alchimie et son livre muet*. Originally published in 1677. Paris: J. J. Pauvert, 1967.

Caprotti, Erminio. *Mostri, draghi e serpenti nelle silografie dell'opera di Ulisse Aldrovandi e dei suoi contemporanei*. Milan: Gabriele Mazzotta Editore, 1980.

Cavendish, Margaret. "The Convent of Pleasure: The Sea-Goddess." In *Seventeenth Century Lyrics*. Edited by Norman Ault. London: Sloane Associated, 1950.

Cerquand, J. F. *Etudes de Mythologie grecque: Les Sirènes*. Paris: Didier et Cie., 1873.

Chailley, Jacques. *Nombres et symboles dans le langage de la musique*. Paris: Comptes-rendus de l'Académie des Inscriptions et Belles Lettres, 1954.

Charbonneau-Lassay, L. *Le Bestiaire du Christ*. Paris: L. J. Toth, 1960.

———. *Etudes de symbologie chrétienne*. Paris: Gutenberg Reprints, 1981.

Chateaubriand, René de. *Génie du Christianisme, Des cloches, Tombeaux*. Paris: Librairie Gamier Frères, 1926.

Cicero. *Opere politiche e filosofiche: I termini estremi del bene e del male*. A cura di Nino Marinone. Turin: Utet, 1953.

Cirlot, Juan Eduardo. *Diccionario de símbolos tradicionales*. Barcelona: Ed. Luis Miracle, 1958.

Clébert, Jean-Paul. *Bestiaire Fabuleux*. Paris: Ed. Albin Michel, 1971.

Colli, Giorgio. *La sapienza greca*. Milan: Adelphi, 1977.

Colon, Cristóbal. *Los cuatro viajes del Almirante y su testamento*. Madrid: Ed. Austral/Espasa Calpe, 1964.

Corpé, Philippe. *Les animaux météo*. Paris: Balland, 1982.

Creuzer, Georg Friedrich. *Philologie*. n.l.: n.p., 1890.

Cumont, Franz. *Le mosaïque de Cherchel figurant Ulysse et lea Sirènes*. Paris: Comptes-rendus de l'Académie des Inscriptions, 1941.

D'Annunzio, Gabriele. *Alcyone*. Brescia: Il Vittoriale degli Italiani, 1939.

D'Arrigo, Stefano. *Horcynus Orca*. Milan: Arnaldo Mondadori Editore, 1982.

Debidour, V. H. *Le bestiaire sculpté du Moyen Age en France.* Schémas d'Edouard Chapotat. Paris: Arthaud, 1961.

Delatte, Armand. *Etudes sur la littérature pythagoricienne.* Paris: Champion Ed., 1915.

Detienne, Marcel. *Les jardins d'Adonis: La mythologie des aromates en Grèce.* Paris: Ed. Gallimard, 1972.

Dinnerstein, Dorothy. *The Mermaid and the Minotaur.* New York: Harper and Row, 1963.

Donne, John. *Selected Poems.* Bell Garden, Calif.: Phoenix Press, 2003.

Douglas, Norman. *Siren Land.* New York: Penguin Books, 1948.

Duchartre, Pierre-Louis. *Imagerie populaire russe.* Paris: Grand, 1961.

Duchaussoy, Jacques. *Le bestiaire divin on la symbolique des animaux.* Paris: Le Courrier du livre, 1972.

Durand, Gilbert. *L'immaginazione simbolica.* Rome: Ed. Il Pensiero Scientifico, 1977.

———. *Le strutture antropologiche dell'immaginario.* Ban: Ediz. Dedalo, 1972.

Durand, José. *Ocaso de Sirenas esplendor de manatíes.* Mexico: Fondo de Cultura Economica, 1950.

Eliade, Mircea. *Images et symboles: Essais sur le symbolisme magico-religieux.* Paris: Gallimard, 1952.

Eliot, T. S. *Selected Poems.* New York: Harvest Books, 1967.

Ellis, Havelock. *Studies in the Psychology of Sex.* London: William Heinemann, 1933.

Elster, Jon. *Ulysses and the Sirens.* London: Cambridge University Press, 1979.

Erasmus of Roterdam. "Enchiridion militis christiani." In *Il Materiale e l'Immaginario* no. 4, Ed. Loescher.

Euripides. "Helena." In *Le diciannove tragedie.* Rome: n.p., 1954.

Faral, Edmond. "La queue de poisson des Sirènes." In *Romania,* t. LXXIV. 1953.

Fiedler, Leslie. *Freaks: Myths and Images of the Secret Self.* New York: Simon & Schuster, 1978.

Freud, Sigmund. *The Interpretation of Dreams.* New York: Avon, 1980.

Fulcanelli. *Le dimore filosofali e il simbolismo ermetico nei suoi rapporti con l'arte sacra e l'esoterismo della Grande Opera.* Rome: Ed. Mediterranee, 1973.

Furlani, Giuseppe. *La religione babilonese e assira.* Bologna: Ed. Nicola Zanichelli, 1928.

Giraudoux, Jean. "Ondine." In *Sipario* no. 126. October 1956.

Gould-Pyle. *Teratologia: Casi clinici.* Turin: Ediz. Universitarie, 1955.

Grandville. *Un autre monde, transformations, visions, incarnations.* Paris: Ed. H. Fourniel, 1844.

Graves, Robert. *The Greek Myths.* New York: Penguin, 1993.

Greenwalt, H. "Come cantano gli uccelli." In *Le Scienze* no. 338, 1975.

Grimm, Jacob and Wilhelm. *Grimm's Complete Fairy Tales.* New York: Barnes & Noble Books, 2001.

Groddeck, Georg. *The Book of the It.* New York: New American Library, 1961.

Guenon, René. *Simboli della scienza sacra.* Milan: Adelphi, 1975.

Guido de Columnis. *Historia destructionis Troiae.* Compiled by Nathaniel E. Griffin. Cambridge, Mass.: The Mediaeval Academy of America, 1936.

Hall, Alice. "Man and Manatee." In *The National Geographic Magazine,* September 1984.

Halleux, Robert. "L'oro potabile." In *Kos.* Franco Maria Ricci, March 1985.

Hamel, Frank. *Animali umani.* Rome: Ediz. Mediterranee, 1974.

Harrison, Jane E. "Monuments Relating to 'The Odyssey.'" In *Journal of Helenic Studies,* 1883.

Hartman, D. S. "Florida's Manatees: Mermaids in Peril." In *The National Geographic Magazine,* vol. 136, no. 3, 1965.

Haspels, Caroline Henriette Emilie. *Attic Black Figured Lekytoi.* Paris: E. De Boccard, 1936.

Heine, Heinrich. *Il libro dei canti.* Turin: Einaudi, 1962.

——. *Nam, elfi e salamandre.* Milan: Facchi Edit., 1965.

——. *Poesie.* Milan: Ed. Riccardo Ricciardi, 1963.

Heraclite. *Allegoria Uomo: Cose mirabili.* Florence: La Nuova Italia, 1965.

Herstal, Stanislaw. *Imagens religiosas do Brasil.* Sao Paulo: Edito Dall'A, 1956.

Hesiod. *Teogonia.* Translated by Cesare Pavese. Turin: Einaudi, 1981.

Heucher, Julius. *A Psychiatric Study of Myths and Fairy Tales.* Springfield: C. Thomas, 1974.

Heuvelmans, Bernard. *Dans le sillage des monstres marines.* Paris: Plon, 1958.

Hillman, James. "An Essay on Pan." In *Pan and the Nightmare.* New York: Spring Publications, 1972.

Homer. *The Odyssey.* Translated by Alexander Pope. New York: The Heritage Press, 1942.

Honorius d'Autun. *Speculum Ecclesiae,* Pl. 172, 855 Cd.

Horace. *Satires, Epistles and Ars Poetica.* Translated by H. Rushton Fairclough. Cambridge: Harvard University Press, 1978.

Horkheimer, Max, and Theodor Adorno. *Dialectic of Enlightenment.* Translated by John Cumming. New York: Herder and Herder, 1972.

Ibsen, Henrik. *La donna del mare.* Florence: Ed. Sansoni, n.d.

Israël, Lucien. *L'hystérique, le sexe et le médecin.* Paris: Masson, 1979.

Jalabert, Denise. "De l'art oriental antique à l'art roman: les Sirènes." In *Bulletin Monumental,* vol. 95. Paris: A. Picard, 1936.

Joanne da Cuba. *Hortus Sanitatis: De Piscibus.* Maguncia: n.p., 1491.

Joyce, James. *Ulysses.* New York: New Random House, 1961.

Jung, Carl Gustav. *Archetypes of the Collective Unconscious.* Princeton, N.J.: Princeton University Press, 1969.

————. *The Psychology of the Unconscious.* London: Routledge & Kegan Paul, 1951.

————. *Paracelsus.* In *Collected Works of C. G. Jung,* vol. 15. Princeton, N.J.: Princeton University Press, 1966.

————. *Psychology and Alchemy.* London: Routledge, 1944.

Jung, Carl Gustav, and Cároly Kerenyi. *Essays on a Science of Mythology.* Princeton, N.J.: Princeton University Press, 1969.

Kafka, Franz. "The Silence of the Sirens." In *The Great Wall of China.* Translated by Willa and Edwin Muir. New York: Schocken Books, 1970.

Kappler, Claude. *Mostri, demoni e meraviglie.* Milan: Ediz. Sansoni, 1983.

Kastner, Georges. *Les Sirènes, Essai sur les principaux mythes relatifs à l'incantation, les enchanteurs, la musique magique, le chant du cigne.* Paris: Imprimeur L. Martinet, 1858.

Keats, John. *The Complete Poems.* New York: Penguin, 1977.

Kerenyi, Cároly. *The Gods of the Greeks.* London: Thames & Hudson, 1980.

————. *The Heroes of the Greeks.* London: Thames & Hudson, 1997.

Kircher, Athanasius. *De arte magnetica,* Book III. Rome: Tipografia Ludovici Grignani, 1641.

Klossowski de Rola, Stanislas. *Alchemy.* London: Thames and Hudson, 1973.

Landrin, Armand. *Les monstres marins.* Paris: Hachette, 1870.

Lautréamont, Isidore Duchasse Compte de. *Les Chants de Maldoror.* Milan: Feltrinells, 1978.

Laysterie, R. de. "Miniatures inédites de l'Hortus Deliciarum." In *Gazette Archéologique,* t. X, 1885.

Leclerc, Jacqueline. "Sirènes-poissons romanes." In *Revue Belge d'Archéologie et d'Histoire de l'Art,* vol. XL. Brussels, 1973.

Leopardi, Giacomo. *Operette morali: Elogio degli Uccelli.* Tuscany: Soc. Edit., 1929.

Lima, Jorge de. *Obra poética.* Rio de Janeiro: n.p., 1967.

Locke, John. *An Essay Concerning Human Understanding.* New York: Oxford University Press, 1979.

Lopez Valdés, Rafael. *Componentes africanos en el etnos cubano.* La Habana: Edit. Ciencias Sociales, 1985.

Luciani Samosateni. "De Syria Dea." *Operum,* t. III. Basel: Gilberti Cognati et Ioannis Sambuci Annotationibus, n.d.

Lucrezio Caro, Tito. *De rerum natura,* V. Florence: Sansoni, 1969.

Luke, David, trans. *Goethe Faust Part Two.* New York: Oxford University Press, 1994.

Lussu, Joyce. *Il libro Perogno: Su donne, streghe e sibille.* Ancone: Il Lavoro Editoriale, 1982.

Malaparte, Curzio. *The Skin.* Translated by David Moore. Marlboro, Vt.: The Marlboro Press, 1988.

Male, Emile. *L'art religieux du XII siècle en France.* Paris: Armand Cohn, 1922.

Mandeville, John. *The Travels of Sir John Mandeville.* New York: Dover, 2006.

Markale, Jean. *Eleanor of Aquitaine.* Rochester, Vt.: Inner Traditions, 2007.

Martial. *Epigrammes,* III, 64, 1. Paris: Ed. Les Belles Lettres, 1950.

Martin, Ernest. *Des monstres depuis l'antiquité a nos jours.* Paris: Reinwald et Cie., 1880.

Masson, Hervé. *Dictionnaire initiatique.* Paris: Ed. Pierre Belfond, 1970.

Maurras, Charles. "Le Mystère d'Ulysse: Le Chant de la Sirène." In *Poètes Contemporains.* Paris: Firmin-Didot, 1938.

Mermaids. The Envelope Library. La Jolla, Calif.: The Green Tiger Press, 1982.

Milton, John. *Paradise Lost,* Book II, v. 829–830.

Monestier, Martin. *Les Monstres: Le fabuleux univers des oubliés de Dieu.* Paris: Tchou, 1978.

Moro, America, and Mercedes Ramirez. *La Macumba.* Montevideo: Ed. de la Banda Oriental, 1981.

Motte-Fouqué, Friedrick de la. *Ondina.* Turin: Ed. Einaudi, 1975.

Nash, Roy. "Meremaides Be Here." In *Coming Events in Britain.* London: British Travel Association, March 1964.

Neruda, Pablo. *Confieso que he vivido: Memorias.* Buenos Aires: Ed. Losada, 1974.

Neumann, Erich. *The Great Mother.* Princeton, N.J.: Princeton University Press, 1972.

Noury, Maurice. "Il compagno di Ulisse." In *Il Mattino Illustrato.* Naples: 12 September 1932.

Ortiz Oderigo, Néstor. *Macumba, Culturas africanas en el Brasil.* Buenos Aires: Ed. Plus Ultra, 1976.

Ovid. *Metamorphoses,* v. 531. Rome: n.p., 1954.

Paracelso. *Traité des Nymphes, Sylphes, Pygmées, Salamandres et autres Etres.* Paris: H. Daragon Ed., n.d.

Pardo Bazan, Emilia. *La Sirena negra.* Madrid: Ed. Aguilar, 1908.

Pascoli, Giovanni. "Poemi conviviali: L'ultimo viaggio." In *Guida al Novecento di S. Guglielminetri*. Milan: Principato Ed., 1971.

Pausanius. *Descrizione della Grecia: Beoticis*. Ed. Spiro, IX 34, 3; X 5, 12.

Pavese, Cesare. *Dialoghi con Leucó: Schiuma d'onda*. Turin: Einaudi Ed., 1947.

Petrarca, Francesco. *Canzoniere: Sonetto CLXVII*. Milan: Ed. Feltrinelli, 1979.

Pettazzoni, Raffaele. *La Confessione dei peccati*. Bologna: Zanichelli Ed., 1935.

————. *Miti e leggende*. Turin: Utet, 1959.

————. *Mitologia giapponese*. Bologna: Zanichelli Ed., 1929.

Phillpotts, Beatrice. *Mermaids*. New York: Ballantine Books, 1980.

Physiologus. Milan: Ed. Adelchi, 1973.

Picard, Charles. "Sur l'Atargatis-Derketo des Thermes d'Aphrodisias en Carie." In *Latomus* vol. II, *Hommages à Bidez et à Cumont*. Brussels: n.p., n.d.

————. "Néreides et Sirènes: Observations sur le folklore hellénique de la mer." In *Annales de l'Ecole des Hautes Etudes de Gand*, T. II, 1938.

Plato. "Republic." In *The Collected Dialogues of Plato*. Edited by Edith Hamilton. Princeton, N.J.: Princeton University Press, 1978.

Pliny. *Natural History*, X, 49 "Sirens"; IX, 4 "Nereids"; and III, 62 "Naples." Translated by John Bostock and H. T. Riley. London: Bohn, 1885.

Plutarch. *Moralia (Quaestiones conviviales)*. Rome: n.p., 1954.

Porphyrius. "Pyrhagorae vita." Appended to Diogenes Laertius, *De clarorum philosophorum vitis*. Paris: n.p., 1850.

Poliziano, Angelo. *Rispetto n. 2: Stanza Polifemo e Galatea*.

Prêle-Timmory, A. "La légende de Mélusine." In *Miroir de l'Histoire*, N. 125. May, 1960.

Propp, V. J. *Le radici storiche dei racconti di fate*. Turin: Boringhieri, 1972.

Provenzal, Dino. *Dizionario delle Immagini*. Milan: Hoepli, 1953.

Prunières, Henri. *Le ballet de cour en France*. Paris: Henri Laurens Ed., 1914.

Pugliese-Carratelli, G. "Orphikòs bios." In *Il Veltro* N. 3. Rome: n.p., 1976.

Quilici, Folco. *Uomini e mari*. Milan: Ed. Mondadori, 1976.

Quintavalle, A. C. *La cattedrale di Modena*. 2 vols. Modena: n.p., 1965.

Rahner, Hugo. *Greek Myths and Christian Mystery*. Cheshire, Conn.: Biblo-Moser, 1963.

Ramorino, Felice. *Mitologia classica*. Milan: Hoepli, 1908.

Reinach, Salomon, and Edmond Pottier. *Nécropole de Myrina*. Paris: Ed. École Francaise d'Athènes/Ernest Thorin, 1887.

Reinach, Salomon. *Répertoire de la statuaire grecque et romaine*. Paris: Ernest Leroux Éd., 1898.

Reistap, J. B., and H. V. Rolland, eds. *Armorial General*. The Hague: Martinus Nijhoff, 1926.

Renesse, Théodore. *Dictionnaire des figures héraldiques.* Brussels: Société Belge de Librairie, 1894.

Ribeiro, René. *Cultos afro-brasileiros de Recife: um estudo de ajustamento social.* Recife: Instituto Joaquim Nabuco de Pesquisas Sociais, 1978.

Ripa, Cesare. *Iconologia.* Venice: Stampato da Cristoforo Tomasini, 1645.

Robinet, J. B. *Vue philosophique de la gradation naturelle des formes de l'être ou Les essais de la Nature qui apprend à faire l'homme.* Amsterdam: n.p., 1768.

Roheim, Géza. *Le porte del sogno: La discesa degli inferi.* Rimini: Guaraldi Ed., 1973.

Ronsard, Pierre de. *Poems.* Translated and edited by Nicholas Kilmer. Los Angeles: University of California Press, 1979.

Rosso, Corrado. *Il serpente e la sirena.* Naples: Ed. Scientifiche Italiane, 1972.

Salmi, Mario. *Chiese romaniche de la campagna toscana.* Milan: Ed. Electa, 1958.

Savi-Lopez, Maria. *Nei Paesi del Nord: Danimarca e Islanda.* Turin: G. B. Paravia, 1923.

Schneider, Marius. *Pietre che cantano: Studi sul ritmo di tre chiostri catalani di stile romanico.* Milan: Ed. Arché, 1976.

Schort. *Physica curiosa,* ch. III. Nurenberg: n.p., 1667.

Schuré, Edouard. "The Sacred Drama of Eleusis." In *Genesis of Tragedy and the Sacred Drama of Eleusis.* Whitefish, Mont.: Kessinger, 1942.

Seneca. *Medea.* Urbin: Soc. Ed. Siciliana, 1956.

Seppilli, Anita. *Poesia e magia.* Turin: Piccola Biblioteca Einaudi, 1962.

———. *Sacralità dell'acqua e sacrilegio dei ponti.* Palermo: Sellerio Ed., 1977.

Servius Gramaticus. *Commento all'Eneide,* V 864–1230. Leipzig: Ed. Thilo et Hagen, 1902.

Shakespeare, William. *Complete Works of William Shakespeare.* New York: Doubleday, 1949.

Shepard, Katharine. *The Fish-tailed Monster in Greek and Etruscan Art.* New York: n.p., 1940.

Siculus, Diodorus. *Bibliotheca,* II, 4. Translated by C. H. Oldfather. New York: G. P. Putnam's Sons, 1933.

"Sirènes d'alerte." In *Lectures pour tons,* N. 18. Paris, June 1918.

Solier, René de. *L'Art fantastique.* Paris: Jean-Jacques Pauvert, 1961.

Storia di Napoli. Naples: Società Editrice Storia di Napoli, 1961.

Storm, Alfonsina. In *Los mejores poemas de la poesía argentina.* Buenos Aires: Ed. El Corregidor, 1974.

Sophocles. *Frammenti* 348, III 861. Rome: n.p., 1954.

Taruffi, Cesare. *Storia delta teratologia,* t. VII. Bologna: Regia Tipografia, 1894.

Tasso, Torquato. *La Gerusalemme Liberata,* IV 86, and XIV 57. Florence: Felice Le Monnier, 1853.

Telliamed on Entretiens d'un philosophe indien avec un missionaire français sur la diminution de la mer. The Hague: le Consul de Maillet, 1775; Paris: Editions Fayard, 1984.

Tomasi di Lampedusa, G. *Two Stories and a Memory: The Professor and the Siren.* Translated by Archibald Colquhoun. London: Collins and Harvil Press, 1986.

Touchefeu-Meynier, Odette. *Thèmes odysséens dans l'art antique.* Paris: Ed. E. de Boccard, 1968.

Turchi, Nicola. *Manuale di Storia delle Religioni.* Turin: Fratelli Bocca, 1912.

Valton, Edmond. *Les monstres dans l'art.* Paris: Flammarion, 1915.

Varano, Giovanni. *Polonia tradita: La Sirena della Vistola.* Rome: Edicoop, 1980.

Veillard-Troiejouroff, May. "Sirènes-poissons carolingiennes." In *Cahiers Archéologiques,* vol. XIX. Paris: Ed. Klincksieck, 1969.

Vernant, Jean-Pierre. "L'immagine della morte nella letteratura e nelle arti figurative." Conferenza École Française de Rome, March 1982.

Vian, Boris. *Textes et chansons: L'évadé.* Paris: Ed. René Juillard, 1966.

Valentine, Basil. *Azoth ou Le moyen de faire l'or caché des Philosophes.* Paris: Pierre Moet Libraire Juré, 1659.

Vigouroux, F. *Dictionnaire de la Bible.* Paris: Letouzey et Ané Ed., 1912.

Vilariño, Idea. *Nocturnos del pobre amor.* Avana: Casa de las Americas, 1989.

Virgil. *The Aeneid.* Rome: Gremese Editore, 1965.

Vitruvio. *Les dix livres d'Architecture.* Paris: Les Libraires Associés, 1965.

Weicker, Georg. *Der Seelenvogel in der alten litteratur and kunst.* Leipzig: Druck und Verlag von B. G. Teubner, 1902.

Wells, H. G. *The Sea Lady.* London: n.p., 1902.

White Muscarella, Oscar. "The Oriental Origin of the Siren Cauldron Attachments." In *Hesperia, Journal of the American School of Classical Studies at Athens,* XXXI, 4, 1962.

Whitman. Walt. *Leaves of Grass.* New York: Doubleday. 1954.

Wilcock, Rodolfo. *Lo stereoscopio dei solitari: La Sirena.* Milan: Ed. Adelphi, 1972.

Wilde, Oscar. *Fairy Tales: The Fisherman and His Soul.* Illustrations by Charles Mozley. London: The Bodley Head, 1960.

Willemsen, Carl Arnold. *L'enigma di Otranto: Il mosaico pavimentale del presbitero Pantaleone nella cattedrale.* Lecce: Congedo Editoriale, 1980.

Willpert, Joseph. *La fede nella Chiesa nascente: Monumenti dell'arte funeraria antica.* Vatican City: n.p., 1938.

Wright, Thomas. *Histoire de la caricature et du grotesque dans la littérature et dans l'art.* Paris: Ed. Adolphe Delahays, 1875.

Yeats, W. B. *Irish Fairy and Folk Tales.* New York: Dorset Press, 1987.

———. *The Poems*. Vol. 1, *The Collected Works of W. B. Yeats*. Edited by Richard
J. Finneran. New York: Macmillan, 1989.

———. *The Collected Plays*. New York: MacMillan, 1952.

Yourcenar Marguerite. *Oriental Tales: The Man Who Loved the Nereids*. Translated by Alberto Manguel in collaboration with the author. New York: Farrar
Strauss Giroux, 1985.

Index

Note: Illustrations are indicated by italic page numbers.

Achelous, 25, 100
Achilles, 30
active listening, 205
Adam, 98, 122
adaptability, 145
Adorno, Theodor W., 90
advertising, 92, 203, 213
Aeneid (Virgil), 58
Albert the Great, 123–24
alchemical symbolism, 123, 150
alchemy, 13, 76, 122
Aldrovandi, Ulisse, 189
Alexander the Great, *101,* 101–3, 183
Alfonso III, King, 181
Allegory of Man (Heraclitus), 41
alphabet, invention of, 52
Amado, Jorge, 142
Ambrose of Milan, 63
Anacreon, 37
Anaximander, 22
Andersen, Hans Christian, 160
angels, 62, 65
anima, the, 16, 36, 41
Anima Mercurii, 123
Anima Mundi, 124
anthropology, psychoanalytical, 38
Aphrodite, 8, 25–26, 33, 96, 130

Apkallu, 95
Apollinaire, Guillaume, 82, 205
Apollo, 46, 48–51, 124
Apollonius of Rhodes, 6, 26, 31, 50
Apsaras, 98
Arcades (Milton), 73
Argolis, 21
Argonautica (Apollonius), 6, 24
Argonauts, 7–8, 49, *61*
Aristotle, 54, 58, 93, 191
Artemis, 28, 100
Art of Poetry (Horace), 104
asiento ceremony, 140
Astarte, 96
Atargatis, 95
Athena, 25, 51, 100
Athenaeus, 48
Augustine, 64
Avicenna, 191
Azoth des Philosophes (Valentine), 123

bablawos, 138, 140
Bachelard, Gaston, 24, 37
Bachofen, J. J., 11, 51
Baltrusaïtus, Jurgis, 13, 93
Barca, Calderón de la, 74
Barnum, P. T., 194, *195*
Baudoin, Jean, 117
Baudrillard, 53
Beaujoyeux, Balthazard de, 117

Beauvais, Vincent de, 182

Beauvoir, Simone de, 37

Becoming, quality of, 22

Being, quality of, 22

Bestiare (Apollinaire), 205

Bestiare d'Amour (Fournival), 113

Bestiare de l'Arsenal, 114

Bestiare Divin (le Clerc), 113

Bestiare (le Picard), 70

bestiaries, medieval, 69, *106,* 106–7

Bible, 60–61, 63

Bibliotheca (Siculus), 96

birth, 22, 25, 33, 36–39, 37

Blanchot, Maurice, 45

Bolen, Jean Shinoda, 100

Bonaparte, Marie, 39

Brant, Sebastian, 185

Brendan, Saint, 181

Bril, Jacques, 128

Browning, Robert, 78

Brussels Manuscript, 61

Buch der Natur (Magenberg), 185

Cabala, 63

Camasenes, 99

Cambridge Bestiary, The, 69–70, 114, *116*

Camus, Albert, 207

Cantimpré, Thomas de, 182

Capricorn, 100

Carracci, Annibale, 3

Cavendish, Margaret (Duchess of Newcastle), 155–56

Celtic legends of Ulster, 80–81

Cerquand, 47, 63

Charles IX, King, 118

Charles V, King of Spain, 186

Charlevoix, 186

cherubim, 62

Chiron, 7

Chorus Phorci, 103

Christ, 45, 61, 63

Christianity, 64

Cicero, 58

Circe, 3–5

Circe (Balthazard), 118

Claudianus, 60

Clébert, Jean-Paul, 186

Clement of Alexandria, 62, 63

collective unconscious, 36

Colli, Giorgio, 21, 126

Columbus, Christopher, 185, *187*

Columnis, Guido de, 115–16

Comedy of Errors (Shakespeare), 154

Company of Fisherman, The, 105, *106*

Comus (Milton), 73

Congal, Saint, 105

cornucopia, origins of, 25

Creuzer, 99

Cuba, Joanne da, 185

dances, ritual, 13

D'Annunzio, 20

Dante, 70–71, 115

dark ladies, 134, 136

d'Arras, Jean, 145

Dea Syria, 96

death, 5, 16–19, 22, 24, 36–40, 208, 220

Debussy, Claude, 179

deceit, 70, 127

Delphina, 145

Demeter and Persephone, myth of, 33–37

"De Piscibus" (Cuba), 185

Derceto, *95,* 96, 119

De Rerum Natura (Cantimpré), 182

devils, 97, 100, 107

Dialectic of Enlightenment (Adorno and Horkheimer), 90–92
Dillon, William, 192
Dinnerstein, Dorothy, 11
Dionysian mysteries, 40
Dionysius of Areopagite, 60
Dionysus, 21, 126, 131
Doctor Moreau (Wells), 167
dog days, 19–20, 54, 100, 136
dolphins, 26, 30–31, 93, 124, 203
Douglans, Norman, 81
dreams, 124
dual natures, 11, 94, 205–6
dugongs, 197, *200*
Durand, Gilbert, 129, 133
Durand, José, 207

Ea, 94–95, 100
Echidna, 97, 145
Egyptians, 17
eight, the number, 57
Eleanor of Aquitaine (Queen), 147
Eleusynian mysteries, 36, 40
El golfo de las Sirenas (Barca), 74
Eliade, Mircea, 13
Eliot, T. S., 160
Ellis, Havelock, 197
Elster, Jon, 92
Emblems (Baudoin), 117
"Endymion" (Keats), 76
Englishman in Italy, Piano di Sorrento, The (Browning), 78
Enlightenment, the, 91
Eos, 3
Erasmus of Rotterdam, 72
Eros, 130
eroticism, 39, 62, 65, 105, 130
eschatological destiny, 33
Etymologies, The (Isidor), 65

Euripides, 35
Eurydice, 49
Eurynome, 2
Eustathius, Bishop of Thessalonica, 66, 67, 69
Eve, 98, 122
evolution, theory of, 195

Fates, 8, 43–44
Faust (Goethe), 76
Feijóo, Benito Jonimo, 191
feminine, the, 32–39, 50, 53, 97–100, 132, 136
fertility goddesses, 96
figureheads on ships, 117, 177
"Fisherman and His Soul, The" (Wilde), 165–67, *166*
Fleurs du Mal (Beaudelaire), 135
four, the number, 42
Fournival, Richard de, 113

Gaea, 26
Gaza, Theodorus, 183
Geography (Strabo), 57
Gervais, 113
Gessner, Conrad, 187
Giamblico, 41
Gilgamesh, 17
gnosis, 63
Goddesses in Everywoman (Bolen), 100
Goethe, Johann Wolfgang, 76
Graves, Robert, 19
Greek musical system, 42
Grimal, Pierre, 33

Hades, descent into, 24
Hamlet (Shakespeare), 105, 154
Harpies, 3, 8, 29, 71

Hathor, 96

Henriquez, Reverend, 193

Hera, 47

Heraclitus, 10, 22, 41

heraldry, 109, *110,* 117, 180, 201

Hermes, 15

Herrad of Landsberg, 66–67

Hesiod, 29, 47

Heuvelmans, Bernard, 198

Hic sunt sirenae, 117

Hillman, James, 20

Hinduism, 94, 98

Hippolytus, 63

Historia Monstrorum (Aldrovandi),
    189

Historia Naturalis (Pliny), 58

Homer, 3, 19, 21, 24, 30

Honoré d'Autun, 66–67

Horace, 103

Horkheimer, Max, 90

Hortus Deliciarum (Herrad), 67, *68*

Hortus Sanitatis, 123

Hudson, Henry, 190

Iconologia (Ripa), 127

Iliad, The (Homer), 22

illusions and illusionism, 40, 127,
    136

immortality, 22, 27, 36, 39, 145

initiation mysteries, 24

International Society of
    Cryptozoology, 198

Inuit culture, 136–38

Isidor of Seville, 65, 93

Iskandarname (Ahmedi), 183

Jason, 7

John the Baptist, 95

Jonah, 95

Joyce, James, 83

Jung, Carl G., 13, 36, 123, 125

Kafka, Franz, 86

Kastner, Georges, 195

katabasis, 24

Keats, John, 76–77

kelpies, 106

Kircher, Athanasius, 190

knowledge, 11, 40, 131

Latini, Brunetto, 114, 136

Latour, Cagniard de, 204

le Clerc, Guillaume, 112

Leibniz, 45

le Picard, Pierre, 70

Letters on the Marvels of India
    (Alexander), 102

Libellus de mirabilus Naturae arcani
    (Parvus), *192*

Liber Exceptionum (Victor), 118–19

Liber Monstrorum, 105, 182

Libro, 102

"Lighea" (Tomasi), 172–74

Lilith, 64, *64,* 98

Little Mermaid, The (Andersen),
    160–65

Livre a Venir, Le (Blanchot), 45

Lorraine, Maillet de, 195

"Love Song of J. Alfred Prufrock"
    (Eliot), 160

Lucian, 96

Lucretius, 11, 191

"Lul de Fantenin" (Apollinaire), 82–83

Lussu, Joyce, 99

Lycosthènes, Corradus, 188

Magenberg, Conrad de, 185

Maillet, Benoit de, 194

Malaparte, Curzio, 174
malformations, physical, 196–97
manatees, 197, *198*
mandrakes, 191–92, *192*
Manual of the Christian Soldier (Erasmus), 72
Manuel I, King, 186
manuscripts, illuminated, 109–16
"Man Who Loved the Nereids, The" (Yourcenar), 170–72
"Man Young and Old, A" (Yeats), 158–59
Mar Muerto (Amado), 142
Martial, 59
Mary, Virgin, 98
Maximus, Bishop of Turin, 65
Medea (Seneca), 49
Medusa, 127
Melusine (d'Arras), 145–49, *148*
Mermaid and the Minotaur, The (Dinnerstein), 11
mermaids, 93, 100–108, 105, 152, 154, 190–95
Metamorphoses (Ovid), 27
metamorphosis, 94
metempsychosis, 15, 42
Methodius of Olympus, 63
Midsummer Night's Dream (Shakespeare), 154–55
Milton, John, 73
Miriam, 98
misogyny, 49, 64, 136
Mnemosyne, 40, 47
Monestier, Martin, 191, 193
Monster of Ravena, 187, *188*
monstrum fascinans, 90
moon, 42, 100, 136
Morrigan, 152

Mother Right (Bachofen), 11
Motte-Fougué, Friedrich de la (Baron), 150
Murgen, 105
Muses, 26, 32, 46, 51
music
    instruments, 9, 19, 41, 131
    knowledge and, 45, 48, 58, 63, 126, 206
    mathematical relationships and, 40, 42, 45
    Muses and, 47
    octaves, 43
    Orpheus and, 6–8, 48–50
    Sirens and, 5, 19, 27, 42–45, 48, 52, 65, 117, 179
    of the spheres, 41
Mutus Liber, 123
mystery religions, 40

Navigatio Brendani, 181
Nemesis, 3
Nereids, the, 27, 105
Neruda, Pablo, 177
Neumann, Erich, 130
New Essays on Human Understanding (Leibniz), 45
Noury, Maurice, 87–89

Odyssey, The (Homer), 3, 22, 24
Olaf of Norway, King, 106
olbophobia, 90
ondinism, 197
On Monsters, Both Terrestrial and Marine, and Their Portraits (Paré), 189
"On Sitting Down to Read *King Lear* Once Again" (Keats), 77
Oracle of Delphi, 42

Orientalis Sive Hierosolymitana Historia (Vitry), 70
Oriental Tales (Yourcenar), 170–72
Orpheus, 6–8, 24, 40, 48, 49, 50, 117
Orphic Argonautica, 10, 48
Orphic mysteries, 40
Orphism, 40, 64
Orungá, 138
Osbern, 181
Otia Imperialis (Gervais), 113
Ovid, 27, 35, 127

Paracelsus, 149–50
Paré, Ambroise, 189
Parmenidean time, 45
Parvus, Albertus Lucius, 182, 191
Pascoli, Giovanni, 79
patriarchy, beginnings of, 51
Paul, Saint, 61, 136
Pausanius, 47
Pavese, Cesare, 28
Perez, Palo, 181
Persephone, 33–37, 48, 100
Perseus, 127
Peter Pan, 156–58
Petrarch, 71
Phaedrus (Plato), 16
Phillip II, King of Spain, 186
Philolaus, 42
Physiologous, The (anon), 60–61, 69, 114
Physiologous, The (Brussels manuscript), 113, *114*
Physiologous, The (Isidor), 93
Physiologous, The (School of Rheims), 113
Picard, Charles, 50
Picasso, Pablo, 13
Plato, 16, 19, 26, 37, 42, 44, 49, 70, 100

Pliny the Elder, 58, 93, 180–81
Plutarch, 36, 60
Poliziano, Angelo, 30, 72
Pope, Alexander, 4
Prodigiorum Ac Ostentorum Chronicon (Lycosthènes), 188, *189*
Propertius, 105
Puck, 152
Pythagoras, 40, 41, 47
Pythagoreanism, 42, 64

Quilici, Folco, 132

Ramayana, The, 98
Raphael (Raffaello Sanzio), 30
reincarnation, 5, 16, 40
Renaissance, 72, 108, 117
Republic, The (Plato), 42
Richard the Lion-Hearted, King, 147
Ripa, Cesare, 127
ritines, 197
Robinet, Jean Baptiste, 195
Roheim, Géza, 38
Roman, 102
Roman de Troie (Sainte-Maure, tr. Columnis), 115–16
Rondelet, Guillaume, 185, 188
Rosso, Corrado, 90
Rufus, Quintus Curtius, 101

sacred, the, 13, 17
Saint-Maure, Benoit de, 115
salvation, 40, 63, 65, 97, 120
Santería, 138
Schmidt, Captain John, 190
Sdivonites, 193
"Sea-Goddess, The" (Cavendish), 156
Sea Lady, The (Wells), 167–70
sea powers, defeat of, 50

Sedna, 136–38, *137*

seduction, 19, 53, 92, 131

Seduction (Baudrillard), 53

Seneca, 49

seraphim, 62

Serpente e La Sirena, Il
    (Rosso, Corrado), 90

Servius, 65

sexuality, 53, 65, 130–33, 136

Shakespeare, William, 152

shamanic trance, 17

Ship of Fools (Brant), 185

Siculus, Diodorus, 96

"Silence of the Sirens, The" (Kafka),
    86–87

"Siren, The" (Tomasi), 172–74

*Sirènes, Essai sur les principaux mythes
    relatifs à l'incantation...* (Kastner),
    195

Sirenian cetaceans, 198

Siren Land (Douglas), 81

sirenomelia, 196

Sirens

    in art, 106–18

    bicaudal, 110, 133, 201

    birth of, 105

    causing death, 51, 65, 70, 72, 122

    Celtic, 105

    combs, 125, 129, 130, 142

    death of, 10, 32, 57

    as demons, 18

    dual nature of, 94

    etymology of, 54–55

    genealogy of, 24–27, 93–100

    giving birth, 111, 121

    hair of, 129–30

    in heraldry, *110,* 148

    identification with sensuality, 63

    in illuminated manuscripts, 107, *110*

    immortality of, 27

    knowledge and, 21, 24, 58, 91, 126

    in literary theory, 90–92

    mirrors, 126–27, 142

    music and, 40

    names of, 55–56

    negative representations of, 61, 100

    number of, 55–56

    in popular culture, 201–3

    in religious rites, 136–44

    in Renaissance, 72–75

    silencing of, 49

    song of, 5, 10

    suicides of, 32

    as symbols, 11, 64

    wings of, 10, 20–21, 32–33, 39–40,
        47, 53, 70

sirens, mechanical, 204

Sisinnius of Antinoe, Saint, 97

Skin, The (Malaparte), 174–77

Socrates, 19

Solidonius, 123

"Song of Wandering Aengus, The"
    (Yeats), 159

"Sonnet 167" (Petrarch), 71

"Sonnet 119" (Shakespeare), 152

Sophocles, 36

Speculum Majus (Beauvais), 182

Stauffenberg, Egenoif von, 150

Stella Maris, 98

Stephanus of Byzantium, 32

Storm, Alfonsina, 87–89

Strabo, 57

Sumerians, 17

symbols

    birds, 16–17, 33, 118, 210

    doves, 62, 96

    in dreams, 13, 38

    fish, 95, 96, 100, 106, 110, 119–25

mast, 63, 65, 69
number eight, 57
number four, 42
number three, 62
sea, 39, 65, 67
water, 22, 24–25, 27, 38–39,
    118–21, 125, 129, 136
wax, 65, 69
wombs, 37–39, 133

tattoos, 201
Teatro Crítico Universal (Feijóo), 191
*Telliamed ou Entretiens d'un philosophe
    indien avec un missionnaire français*
    (Maillet), 194
Tertullian, 120
Tesoretto (Latini), 114
Tetractys, the, 42
Thaletes, 22
Thanatos, 18
Theobald, Abbot of Monte Cassino, 65
Theogeny (Hesiod), 47
Thetis, 30–31
three, the number, 62
Toltecs, 17
Tomasi, Giuseppe (Prince of
    Lampedusa), 172
Trismegistus, 45, 123
Tritons, the, 104

Ulysses, 3–6, *8, 9,* 19–20, 24, 25,
    63, 100
Ulysses and the Sirens (Elster), 92
Ulysses (Joyce), 83–84
unconscious, collective, 36
"Undine" (Motte-Fouqué), 150, *151*
undines, 150, *151*
Universum Piscium Historia
    (Rondelet), 185

Valentine, Basil, 123
Valkyries, the, 75–76
Vernant, Jean Pierre, 18
Vesalio, Andrea, 186
Viceroy of Goa, 193
Victor, Saint, 118
Vilariño, Idea, 90
Virgen de Regla, 140
Virgil, 58
Virgin Mary, 98
Vishnu, 94
Vitruvius, 104
Vitry, Jacques de, 70
Voltaire, 195
voyeurism, 127
*Vue philosphique de la gradation
    naturelle des formes de l'etre . . .*
    (Robinet), 195

Water and Dreams (Bachelard), 24
Waterhouse, John William, 1
1823 Weddell Expedition to the
    Antarctic, 193
Wells, H. G., 167
Whitman, Walt, 38
Wilcock, Rodolfo, 177
Wilde, Oscar, 165
wings, 16–17, 40, 93
women, 21, 36, 64, 70, 100, 124, 136,
    197

Yeats, William Butler, 79, 106,
    158–59
Yemanjá, *131,* 131–32, 138–44,
    139
Yourcenar, Marguerite, 170–72

Zeus, 47
zoological specimens, 197